RESTORATIVE PRACTICES THAT HEAL SCHOOL COMMUNITIES

A UNIVERSAL DESIGN FOR LEARNING APPROACH

RESTORATIVE PRACTICES THAT HEAL SCHOOL COMMUNITIES

Mirko Chardin, Pamela Chu-Sheriff, and Edgar Vasquez

© 2025 CAST, Inc.

All rights reserved. No part of this publication may be reproduced, stored in a retrieval system, or transmitted in any form or by any means, electronic, mechanical, photocopying, recording, or otherwise, without the prior permission of the Publisher.

ISBN (paperback): 978-1-943085-12-5
ISBN (ebook): 978-1-943085-13-2

Library of Congress Control Number: 2024949816

Cover and Interior Design: Happenstance Type-O-Rama

Published by CAST Professional Publishing,
an imprint of CAST, Inc.,
Lynnfield, Massachusetts, USA

For information about special discounts for bulk purchases, please email publishing@cast.org or visit publishing.cast.org.

To my amazing wife, Hayley, for your continued support and encouragement. To my mother, Odeline, for being my first and best teacher. To all educators—and anyone working with young people—who value, champion, and honor their voices. To my father, Leandre, and grandmother, Florette, who first taught me the value and power of listening. And lastly, to the ancestors who came before all of us and first brought these ideas and work into the world.

—MIRKO

Jamin and Naomi—somehow, I have been given the greatest of blessings, which is to know you and to have you in my life every single day. I love you. To my parents, James and Christina Chu, I don't know where or who I would be without your love and sacrifice. I will try my best to make you proud.

—PAM

To my son Devin, for giving me the gift and experience of joy! You have always been my inspiration and my greatest blessing. I love you. Keep being AMAZING! To all of my loved ones in my life, my family, those closest to me, and those whom I have known over the years, I learn from each and every one of you, and I am humbled by it. And to Carmen Torres.

—EDGAR

CONTENTS

Introduction 1

PART A: A SCHOOL IN NEED OF HEALING
1: What Had We Done Wrong? 7
2: Our Schools Need Healing 11
3: Defining a Healthy Culture 15
4: Diagnosing Your Culture 21
5: Restorative Practices for Repair and Healing 27
6: Righting a Sinking Ship With Restorative Practices 31
7: Pause and Reflect On Part A 37

PART B: RESTORATIVE PRACTICES, INDIGENOUS ORIGINS
8: It Started Over Pancakes 41
9: What Are Restorative Practices? 45
10: Circle Practice 49
11: Formal Structures 55
12: The Social Discipline Window 59
13: Indigenous Origins 61
14: Restorative Practices in Schools 67
15: A Restorative Journey 71
16: Pause and Reflect On Part B 75

PART C: THE POWER OF STUDENT VOICE
17: Stories of Belonging . . . or Not 79
18: Considering the Recipients of Our Service 85
19: Cogenerative Dialogues (Cogens) 87
20: Steps to Implementing Cogen Groups 93
21: Honoring Student Voices 97
22: Using Restorative Practices for Teaching and Learning 103
23: Using Restorative Practices for Learner Agency: Math Talks . . 109
24: From Finding Voice as a Learner to Finding Voice as a Teacher . . . 115
25: Pause and Reflect On Part C 119

PART D: SOCIAL-EMOTIONAL LEARNING THROUGH PERSONAL NARRATIVES

26: Story Time 123
27: Harnessing the Power of Personal Narratives 127
28: "I Am Because We Are": An Example of Personal Narrative . . . 131
29: Making the Connection to Social-Emotional Learning 137
30: The S.O.D.A. Strategy 147
31: Story of Self: Honoring Students' Identities and
 Social-Emotional Learning 149
32: Pause and Reflect On Part D 157

PART E: CHANGE ISN'T ONE-SIZE-FITS-ALL

33: The Purpose of School Change: Healing and Restoration 161
34: Decolonizing Education, Shifting Mindsets 165
35: Magic Happens, but It's Not a Magic Wand 171
36: Learning From Implementation Science 181
37: A Time for Change: Edgar's Story 185
38: Pause and Reflect On Part E 197

PART F: UNIVERSAL DESIGN FOR LEARNING AND RESTORATIVE PRACTICES

39: What Is Universal Design for Learning? 201
40: The Connection Between UDL and Restorative Practices 211
41: Vision, Values, and Voice 215
42: Returning to the "Why" of Learning 219
43: Community Conversations 231
44: Not Just One More Thing to Do 235
45: Pause and Reflect On Part F 237

APPENDIX: The UDL Guidelines 3.0 239

Acknowledgments 241
Land Acknowledgment 243
References 247
Index 251
About the Authors 265

INTRODUCTION

*Rarely, if ever, are any of us healed in isolation.
Healing is an act of communion.*
—bell hooks, African American feminist and author

You might have heard your colleagues refer to restorative practices or Universal Design for Learning (UDL) in various education spaces, or perhaps you've already attended a professional development training on one of these topics. Perhaps you're thinking, *Aren't restorative practices that thing where everyone sits around in a circle and just talks about their feelings?* (It is so much more than that!) Or maybe you've wondered, *Isn't UDL just the same as backward design?* (Again, it is so much more than that!) We'll first briefly define our terms, and then, most importantly, we'll dive into *why* restorative practices and UDL, and why *now*?

Restorative practices represent both a framework and range of approaches that aim to develop community and relationships and to prevent and repair conflict and harm. UDL is also a framework based on decades of research in neuroscience and learning that empowers educators to proactively plan for barriers in their lesson design, give students voice and choice in their learning, and challenge and support all students, regardless of their differences. Both of these frameworks are student centered, and we will illustrate throughout this text how restorative practices align with UDL's fundamental tenet of providing students with voice and agency. When restorative practices are viewed through a UDL lens, we can expand our conceptual frameworks and add to our educator toolkits to ensure that all students are included, valued, supported, and empowered.

Restorative practices and restorative justice might feel like the latest trends in education. However, these movements have ancient roots, inspired by Indigenous cultures and peoples from around the globe who have been incorporating these principles into their way of being long before the westernized "restorative justice movement" started gaining traction in criminal justice systems in the 1970s (Joe et al., 2022). Although the terms are often used interchangeably, restorative justice is a subset of restorative practices that aims to hold offenders accountable for their wrongs by involving them in repair processes with the people they have harmed. This is an important distinction. Since restorative justice as a movement has its roots in the criminal justice system, we choose to use the term *restorative practices* instead when referring to what happens in schools. It may go without saying that some of our young people are already unfairly criminalized at far too early of an age, so avoiding any language that may reinforce this, even unintentionally, is advisable.

Whether we like it or not, long gone are the days in which a teacher was simply the "sage on the stage," and students' brains were just receptacles to be filled. As Paulo Freire, father of critical pedagogy, writes in *Pedagogy of the Oppressed* (2000): "Liberating education consists in acts of cognition, not transferrals of information" (p. 79). Authentic learning, then, involves sparking and maintaining our students' interest and requires that young people be co-creators in their educational journeys.

As today's students grapple with a myriad of issues brought about by social media, mental health challenges, food insecurity, racism, and societal inequality, to name a few, they need our support now more than ever. As restorative practices teach us, being able to acknowledge hurt is the first step toward healing. When we can give voice to what our students are going through, we can equip them with the tools to build agency and community. What's more, brain science tells us that when students feel a sense of belonging and safety, they learn and process new information more effectively.

Now that we've briefly introduced restorative practices, we'll take a moment to introduce ourselves. Who are we? First and foremost, we are lifelong learners who are humbly sharing with you what we have learned on our journey as educators. As people of color from diverse family backgrounds that include Haiti, Taiwan, and Puerto Rico, we are unapologetic in our commitment to social justice not only in our work but also in how we live our lives each day. For us, the professional *is* personal; we strive to be what we ourselves weren't able to see when we were growing up and struggling with identity, intergenerational trauma, and the various "-isms" that these obstacles may entail. We were all drawn to the field of education to be for our students what we didn't always have in our own schooling—someone who could validate our experiences and who could give us a means to voice those experiences.

Each of us has an average of two decades working deep in the trenches as both classroom teachers and building-based administrators in predominantly urban settings, where, far too often, student voices are left by the wayside or actively stifled. In addition, the three of us have experience as practitioners of both restorative practices and UDL in our respective school settings, having launched restorative practices programs in our schools while utilizing UDL along the way. (We'll address how restorative practices and UDL blend together in Part F.)

Mirko and Pam were the founding head of school and the founding assistant principal, respectively, of the Putnam Avenue Upper School, a public middle school in Cambridge, Massachusetts, that serves predominantly low-income students and students of color from families representing over 25 languages. The school hosted learning tours for district and school administrators from across the state, including the Massachusetts Department of Elementary and Secondary Education (DESE), and across the country. The school was also recognized by the DESE for leading efforts in Massachusetts to establish culturally responsive schools and classrooms and for its use of restorative practices. Mirko and Pam currently serve as education consultants, presenting across the country and internationally on restorative practices and UDL. Edgar has been a long-time educator in the Boston Public Schools (BPS). He currently serves as the founding dean of students at Boston Arts Academy, the only public arts school in Boston. Edgar continues to serve as an administrator there, where his school has been hailed as a model across the district and beyond for its restorative practices program.

Suffice to say, we've spent our careers working with what are considered some of the most "high needs" student populations. We can say with utmost confidence that shifting from teacher-centered to student-centered classrooms and providing students with voice and agency is hands-down one of the most powerful ways to build community and to ultimately open the gateway for authentic learning to take place.

LeVar Burton, host of the beloved children's program *Reading Rainbow*, used the catchphrase, "But you don't have to take my word for it!" before each segment on student book recommendations. As some of you may recall, Mr. Burton would look straight into the camera and repeat this tagline with both cheer and gravitas. Although he was a trustworthy and seasoned expert, his words intimated to viewers, *I can say all I want, but you should really listen to the voices of these young people, and then you can really see for yourself.* We hope you take our word for it, but ultimately, examining or shifting belief systems—coupled with the added work of adjusting practice—is a deeply personal journey that takes a willingness to trust our young people enough to give them space to speak. Doing so involves matters of both the head and the heart, so we invite you to proceed at your own pace and in your own time as you explore this text. We can assure you that the journey will be worth it.

PART A

A School in Need of Healing

Hope deferred makes the heart sick.
—Proverbs 13:12

1

What Had We Done Wrong?

MIRKO CHARDIN

We were in trouble at the Putnam Avenue Upper School and didn't have a clue how we got there or what to do about it. "Crisis" was the word that certain parents, students, faculty, and even some district administrators used to describe what was happening. It was also what the data showed.

We had founded our school just a year earlier, and in building it, we thought we had created an inclusive, welcoming culture. We had developed a vision statement democratically by garnering input from students, parents, caregivers, community members, faculty, and staff. We explicitly stated our belief that all of our young people were on a journey toward the best quality of life in adulthood, and that it was our job as a school community to guide them on this path by exemplifying our five core values (also democratically defined with community input): passion, pride, ownership, balance, and perseverance. By *passion*, we meant academic excellence and social justice that recognized different experiences from race, gender, class, gender identity, sexual identity, and religion. Our idea of *pride* focused on the positive impact that expressing our authentic identities would have on other individuals. We defined *ownership* as everyone in the community taking responsibility for goal setting, planning, decision-making, and fulfillment. We defined *balance* as blending academics with extracurriculars and self-care, and we boldly acknowledged that the work of *perseverance* means not only that we have faced and overcome challenges but also that we've explicitly shared our strategies for doing so.

We also committed to having a staff that reflected our learners, and our staff was extremely diverse. In fact, the state department of education recognized our staff as being the most representative of any schools in the Commonwealth. We committed to being in the building early and staying late, and doing whatever it took to try to reach kids. We had all the right ingredients to support and honor our learners—Black, Brown, Yellow, White, broke, and wealthy. We talked often about how there was nothing we wouldn't do, nothing we wouldn't sacrifice, to support our learners, because we believed in them. We had access to resources in curriculum and professional development; we had access to what seemed like everything and anything we could imagine that would help that work.

Arriving at this place—at least on paper—made us feel pretty good about ourselves and the school community we had created. We had the recipe for success. So why were we in crisis? Why, despite these great intentions and values, was there so much tension in our school?

Students were unhappy with faculty. Faculty seemed to nurture grudges against students—not just individuals, but entire cohorts. The tensions led to numerous office referrals, disciplinary circumstances, and suspensions. A perceived lack of safety and trust permeated the school. Staff were tired, overwhelmed, overburdened, burnt out, and overwhelmed by negativity. Something wasn't working, and things were falling apart.

In a moment of vulnerability and desperation, I took a chance and engaged the school community in *WE Teach* and *WE Learn* surveys from the Successful Practices Network (SPN), which asked adult community members as well as students about their perceptions of the school and what was or wasn't working. The responses from the two groups would then be triangulated. While reviewing the data from the surveys, I found there was one question in particular that dynamically changed who I was as a leader and dynamically changed our school community: "Do you believe that students are well known; treated with respect and dignity; and seen, heard, and well cared for in this space?"

More than 80% of staff overwhelmingly responded with thoughts like the following: *Yes, this is a wonderful place; I love it here; the staff is amazing; we are so committed to students; we care about students; we're here before and after school; our school culture is the thing we do better than anybody else, despite the issues we're currently having.*

The responses from students were also unified—though in the opposite direction: 80% did *not* feel that they were well known, well cared for, or treated with respect and dignity. In fact, they didn't like going to this school.

Sitting with that data was like a gut punch. It was heart-wrenching to see that the students did not agree with our self-assessment that we cared about them and were working hard to communicate that caring. The response from the faculty was emotional. Many said things like, "Why are we even listening to kids? They don't know what they're talking about!" and "They probably weren't taking this seriously. They're probably just trying to do this to make us upset."

The data—showing the truth of how students really felt—did not align with our intentions in any way, shape, or form. This reaffirmed for us that, despite how good we felt about our practices, our job as educators wasn't about intent. Our work had to be about having a positive impact on the hearts, minds, lives, and experiences of those we serve.

One of the most powerful learnings that came from this survey, once we were able to digest and process it, was that we didn't value student voice, and we didn't even realize it. We insisted that we valued it, but we had no systems, structures, or routines to support and ensure learner agency. We needed to understand students' experiences as opposed to just seeing demographic information that purported to represent them. We needed to intentionally design school experiences for students that centered their voices.

We committed to reconfigure our existing structures, systems, rituals, and routines so that students' voices were always at the center. For us, this was key to healing and mending our trust and belief in each other. Restorative practices would help us hear and see each other so that we could heal the hurt and move from being a school community in crisis to one that was thriving.

2

Our Schools Need Healing

Working in schools is not an easy task, and we've written this text to acknowledge that fact and to share—based on lived experiences and not just theory—our knowledge that it is both possible and plausible to heal school communities, districts, and classrooms, which (whether or not we have the courage to acknowledge it) are currently broken. As readers, you are invited to join us on this journey as we share, through the lens of our own personal experiences as well as those of several colleagues across the nation, the power of universally designed restorative practices to transform unhealthy school environments and cultures into thriving ones.

Variability is real, and our experiences at school, good or bad, are not the same. This is extremely evident to Mirko and Pam as we travel the nation to support schools and school communities in our capacity as education consultants. Based on those experiences and travels, here is a glimpse at what a school in need of healing may look like.

All classroom doors open at the same time, and a cascade of students emerges, starting to walk slowly along duct-taped lines that stretch down the corridor. Students stop at each checkpoint along their journey to their next class. Although there are hundreds of students, the hallway is silent except for the shuffling of feet and the random terrifying shouts of "S-Q-F!" from the faculty. S-Q-F, or Single Quiet File, is a transition practice in which students move silently in a single line from one location to another. It places a premium on quiet movement, respect for others, and maintaining a calm environment. Some adults in the corridor are also heard saying, "I wish one would try to get out of line, so we can show them what we do to troublemakers and those who don't follow the rules."

A student drops her bookbag; the noise startles everyone in the corridor, including the adults, who all turn to her with intense glares. "I'm sorry. It's heavy. It fell," she explains. Now sobbing, she quickly picks up the bag and clutches it, mumbling, "I hate it here." A staff member replies, "Little girl! S-Q-F! Pick it up. Keep it moving. We don't need your opinions. We hate it here, too, but as long as I have bills to pay, you're gonna S-Q-F in these halls!"

Now, picture another scenario: A student enters their classroom after being out for a few days. They are neither greeted nor acknowledged by the teacher; they proceed to their seat quietly and sit there. A few days before, there had been a significant classroom disruption involving this student. They had gotten into an intense shouting match with the teacher about the content the class was studying. The teacher had requested that the school administration reprimand and remove the student. The school facilitated a follow-up response to the teacher's request and the student had been cleared to return to the class after their suspension period was up. Now, the student raises their hand and asks for direction about what they missed while they were out. Immediately, the teacher responds with, "Don't talk to me. Sit there and think about what you did!"

As readers, what are your reactions to these circumstances? Do they echo experiences that you have had, witnessed, or participated in as a learner or an educator? Or do they echo experiences that you have heard described by friends, colleagues, or social media posts? Or are they situations and circumstances that you have not encountered or that are surprising to you?

Many of us may agree that there is nothing worse than being in a place that makes you feel uncomfortable. It's even worse if you can tell that the people who work there are also uncomfortable. Sometimes, these are places where we may not feel seen, heard, or acknowledged. They are spaces in which we may feel judged or that we're being treated as "less than" others. Unfortunately, this can be a common occurrence in school buildings and classrooms that have not implemented proactive frameworks, such as Universal Design for Learning (UDL), to ensure that the needs of all individuals are taken into account as a central component of the planning process. We believe that, while neglecting to do so is typically an unintentional misstep by educators, the impact can be devastating, especially when they are not even aware that they're doing it.

Healing means more than implementing quick technical fixes. These are deep-seated problems requiring solutions that go well beyond classroom management tricks and tips, well beyond one meeting or a dry professional development session. We are speaking directly to how the human beings in a space are experiencing each other and how that positively and negatively impacts and sometimes, if left unaddressed, undermines the best of intentions.

Furthermore, we are not absolved through ignorance; in fact, not knowing that your school culture needs healing may indicate that it needs it more than ever. By "school culture," we mean the organizational and systemic culture of schools, and it may need healing regardless of whether you are aware of it. If you do not have intentional systems, structures, rituals, and routines that honor healing and facilitate opportunities for students to listen, learn, and be seen, heard, and understood, your school culture may need healing. If you are not deliberately inclusive, you may be excluding whomever you have not considered in your design process, and your school culture may need healing. If you do not have a purposefully inclusive, welcoming, and safe culture that values voice, then you may not be poised to repair ruptures when conflicts, intentional or not, emerge, and your school culture may need healing.

Currently, many educators and students are experiencing schools as toxic environments and disengaging with school. Many school communities are wrestling with environments that are neither safe nor welcoming, and nationwide academic trends show that learners are disengaged, struggling, involved in inappropriate activities and behaviors, and not coming to school regularly. School attendance rates have fallen so much that in states like Massachusetts, the secretary of education has made personal pleas via television advertisements to ask parents to support getting their children back in school. Educators, feeling burnt out, disrespected, underequipped, and poorly supported, are leaving the profession in droves, leading to nationwide and international staffing shortages.

However, we can mitigate much of this by proactively acknowledging these circumstances and by developing a culture fluent in the use of restorative practices to address them.

Many school communities that have become steeped in the work of equity and providing equitable access to learners are doing this work because of their need for healing. If you are not also steeped in the work of supporting the adults within your community so that they are seen, heard, and treated with respect and dignity, then your school culture may need healing. If there are no mechanisms to gather, normalize, invite, and engage in regular internal and external critical feedback, then your school culture may need healing. Learn from our experience and be intentional about this process: if you're not intentional, the healing can't and won't happen.

3

Defining a Healthy Culture

School culture, as defined by Fullan (2007), refers to the guiding beliefs and values evident in how a school operates. School culture relates to how the school feels as perceived by the individuals who constitute that school community, as well as the rituals, routines, systems, and structures that serve as evidence of both what is and what is not valued. It's about the experience and the emotional interpretation of having membership in that community. The word *culture* can also be defined as a way of life, so when thinking of school culture, think of the school's way of being. A key question to keep in mind is: Is this something that has been developed with some intentionality, or has it developed unintentionally?

Whether we have launched the school or inherited it, we as educators must come to terms with the fact that we are responsible for cultivating and nurturing the existing culture. We are responsible for knowing the practices, the values, how we do things, and how we celebrate (or don't), knowing that decisions and practices sometimes manifest as hidden curriculum, implicit bias, or institutional racism.

Individual classrooms are microcosms of a school's culture and all of the elements, good or bad, that exist within the context of the larger school community. Classroom teachers have the ability to create, nurture, and support the learning environment they work in if they recognize that their job is not to simply deliver content for the sake of content but rather to guide young learners on educational journeys. To do this, educators need to create spaces where learners feel safe and secure, can trust and be courageous, and are appropriately challenged so they will grow and learn. Learners need access to classrooms where they have a sense of self-efficacy and independence. Educators at all levels must provide rich learning experiences that reinforce developing that sense of independence within our customers and clients: our young learners, our kiddos, our students.

Leah Shafer (2018) suggests that culture is shaped by five interwoven elements:

1. **Fundamental beliefs and assumptions**, or the things people at your school consider to be true. For example: "All students have the potential to succeed," or "Teaching is a team sport."

2. **Shared values**, or the judgments people at your school make about those beliefs and assumptions—whether they are right or wrong, good or bad, just or unjust. For example: "It's wrong that some of our kindergarteners may not receive the same opportunity to graduate from a four-year college," or "The right thing is for our teachers to be collaborating with colleagues every step of the way."

3. **Norms**, or how members believe they *should* act and behave, or what they think is expected of them. For example: "We should talk often and early to parents of young students about what it will take for their children to attend college," or "We all should be present and engaged at our weekly grade-level meetings."

4. **Patterns and behaviors**, or the way people *actually* act and behave in your school. For example, there are regularly scheduled parent engagement nights around college; there is active participation at weekly team curriculum meetings (in a weak culture, these patterns and behaviors can be different from the norms).

5. **Tangible evidence**, or the physical, visual, auditory, or other sensory signs that demonstrate the behaviors of the people in your school.

Examples might include prominently displayed posters showcasing the district's college enrollment, or a full parking lot an hour before school begins on the mornings when curriculum teams meet.

IT HAS TO BE INTENTIONAL

Unless we are intentional about equity and cultural responsiveness being central to our organizational culture, they won't be. Discipline practices are typically rooted in our perception of students and not who they actually are despite our best intentions to see them differently. In schools in which the educators do not feel safe, students are often perceived as potential threats. When the work revolves simply around intention and there is no awareness of or correlation to impact, learners and staff feel silent and invisible. There is no trust and low morale. Kids hate that. Adults hate it, too.

When students don't have an adult at their school that they trust, they will simply navigate the school on their own and survive as best as they can. Students require direction and support from their elders, their teachers. A teacher is more than just an educator who facilitates content knowledge. Teachers model healthy relationships while maintaining boundaries and parameters with their students. When a school does not foster healthy relationships between students and teachers, there is no sense of community and no sense of belonging. This circumstance is exacerbated when cafeteria staff, school clerks and secretaries, bus drivers, and custodial staff don't have strong relationships with students.

In responding to student behaviors, many schools operate from a punitive place, normalizing student exclusion from school as a primary response to negative behavior. They decide to remove the "problem" as a means of discipline and of letting other students know what will happen to them if they cause a problem. When students are excluded at a high rate and as a primary response to their behaviors, they develop an identity of low self-worth and a sense of not belonging—a result that can have long-term consequences. To provide a more acute and appropriate intervention, schools must reconsider their approaches and responses to student behaviors and consider students' developmental stages.

IT HAS TO BE ACKNOWLEDGED TO BE ADDRESSED

To heal our school culture, we must first acknowledge that it exists and examine whether or not it is currently facilitating the experiences and outcomes we want. If we determine that it is not, we must acknowledge that and then commit to the journey of exploring why it is the way it is so that we can address the problems. The notion of healing school culture is informed by and grounded in trauma-informed school theory. This educational approach recognizes the profound impact of trauma on students' lives and learning. It emphasizes creating a safe, supportive, and nurturing environment that takes into account the challenges students may have faced and aims to foster resilience, well-being, and academic success by acknowledging and addressing the effects of trauma (Bloom, 2013). The key principles include:

- **Safety first:** Prioritize creating a safe space where students feel physically and emotionally secure.

- **Building trust:** Establish trust through open communication, consistent support, and transparent policies.

- **Choice and empowerment:** Offer students choices and involve them in decisions, promoting a sense of control.

- **Collaborative community:** Foster a sense of belonging by working together with students, families, and colleagues.

- **Skills for life:** Equip students with coping skills and emotional tools for stress management.

- **Cultural sensitivity:** Recognize and respect diverse cultural backgrounds and their impact on students' experiences.

- **Peer support:** Encourage positive peer relationships to create a supportive network.

- **A strengths-based approach:** Focus on students' strengths and resilience, building on their capabilities.

- **Continuous learning:** Provide ongoing training to educators about trauma and its effects.
- **Early intervention:** Identify signs of trauma early and offer appropriate support.

Furthermore, in *Responding to Childhood Trauma*, Hodas (2006) states that "incorporating trauma-informed practices requires collaboration among school staff, families, and the community. By understanding and responding to trauma, educators can create an environment that promotes healing, growth, and successful learning outcomes" (p. 50). The goal of trauma-informed school theory is to provide the best possible support for students, considering their unique experiences and needs, while fostering a positive, empowering, and healing learning environment.

Positive and equitable school cultures are those in which everyone is seen and heard and has a sense of both belonging and agency. Upon entering a school, anyone walking in should be able to feel a welcoming and safe space. Upon further observation, they should see students interacting with one another in healthy and positive ways—holding doors for one another, saying "excuse me," and greeting their peers with a warm or welcoming hug—and adults greeting students by their names, students naturally gravitating toward and engaging with the adults, adults positively interacting with one another, and so on.

We can measure the impact of our current school culture on students by looking at our data, by speaking to students directly, by conducting equity audits, and by developing systems and structures that normalize including their voices. Restorative practices are practices that intentionally restore agency by being a mechanism through which their voices can be shared.

4

Diagnosing Your Culture

Your school culture may need healing. We know this because we are currently living in a society that needs healing. The past several years have been traumatic in ways that our society has not encountered before, and the circumstances have been far-ranging. As human beings, we do not have the ability to separate ourselves from the personal impacts of the trauma we have collectively experienced. Whether we acknowledge it or not, we carry it with us as we navigate our days, colleagues, systems, and students. The need for healing is not solely about a school's student population, but about the adults as well. It's about acknowledging the impact of what we unintentionally bring to school with us and how, unaddressed, it can impact our relationships with colleagues as well as with our learners.

The same phenomenon of trauma impacts youth just as much as it does adults. It is important that we have space to think not only about how the events occurring in our culture and society impact us as educators, but also about what systems, structures, routines, and values will make our schools safe spaces that support our young learners as they navigate the messy world they are sharing and ultimately inheriting from us.

We have to create systems and structures that ensure our schools are safe and welcoming places. Then, we need to make sure to do the work to make them brave spaces as well, meaning they foster a willingness to dig into discomfort, persist, and persevere in the same manner that the UDL principle of engagement directs us to consider options for self-regulation, persistence, and perseverance.

Neuroscience has taught us much about the role of the limbic system—in particular, our amygdala and the role it plays in facilitating the flight, fight, or freeze response when we are riddled with anxiety, full of fear, and/or overwhelmed. As we consider what it takes to create safe, brave, and healing spaces in our school, we must be proactive in designing systems, structures, routines, and rituals that soothe the amygdala rather than trigger it.

We can only do this work when we've committed to go above and beyond access, meaning that we wrestle with the Beyond Access framework (Chardin & Novak, 2020) and its three critical reflective questions:

1. **Valuing impact over intentions:** Are we valuing impact on learners over adult intentions?

2. **Learner representation:** Can all learners see themselves reflected in the work?

3. **Authentic relevance:** Are the learning environment and work authentically relevant for the learners sitting before us?

It may be valuable to reflect on our practices and whether they go beyond access. Table A-1 includes a checklist educators can use to evaluate their lesson plans, teaching strategies, and overall approach. For each criterion, they can mark Yes, Partially, or No based on their analysis. After completing the assessment, they can tally up the points and interpret the results to guide their efforts in creating a more equitable and inclusive learning environment.

Remember, this tool is a starting point, and educators can tailor it to suit their specific context and needs. It's all about fostering a culture of continuous improvement and ensuring that every learner feels valued, represented, and engaged in their educational journey. This tool will help them determine if they are valuing impact over intentions, ensuring learner representation, and achieving authentic relevance.

TABLE A-1: Beyond Access Quick Check Tool

CRITERIA	YES	PARTIALLY	NO
1. Valuing impact over intentions			
Are learning outcomes focused on real-world impact and results?			
Are adjustments based on feedback and student needs?			
2. Learner representation			
Do learning materials and examples reflect diverse identities?			
Are diverse perspectives integrated into discussions and activities?			
3. Authentic relevance			
Are learning experiences connected to students' lives and interests?			
Do students see the practical application of what they're learning?			

Scoring:
- Yes: 2 points
- Partially: 1 point
- No: 0 points

Interpretation:
- 6 points: Excellent! Your planning is highly equitable and inclusive.
- 4–5 points: Good job! Your planning demonstrates a fair level of equity and inclusion.
- 1–3 points: Some improvements needed. Focus on areas with low scores.
- 0 points: Consider revising your planning to be more equitable and inclusive.

Throughout our practices, we have to continually reflect on our culture and climate. We have to commit to identifying the school's blind spots so we can start developing an understanding of how our young people, as well as the members of the school community (administrators, teachers, staff, family, caregivers, and community members), perceive the school.

We then have to dig even deeper to get a sense of what the school experience looks like for different types of students and adults based on demographic information and identity markers so we know whether we truly understand the impact of our system on all stakeholders. To do this, we have to wrestle with the equation of values plus practices equaling outcomes.

We need to look at our outcomes—academic data, high-stakes test data, attendance data, discipline data, and graduation and dropout rates—through these lenses to determine with precision whether or not we're providing equitable circumstances. If that is not the case or we find there's work that needs to be done, we commit to addressing it.

There will be moments of conflict and challenge, but there are mechanisms that we can intentionally put in place beforehand to help us repair ruptures. We have to recognize that these dilemmas will not be the end of our work; they are stumbling blocks that we will learn to transform into stepping stones as we move forward, normalizing the fact that challenge is a part of the work. We must be committed to developing systems, structures, and routines that guide us when we encounter and deal with challenges, knowing that we *will be* successful.

If we believe that all of our learners—the young learners and the adult learners—have the potential to develop learner agency in our school communities, we will design with the expectation that our folks will be successful.

If we believe our learners will be successful at high levels, then having high expectations means that there are certain actions that we take only because we have this belief. It also means normalizing listening to the voices of our learners. If we want greater potential to be manifested within a learning space, we have to design for variability, which means we must create climates and cultures maintained through systems, structures, routines, and rituals that empower us and provide opportunities for us to redesign structures and actions in real time.

Peter Senge (1990), in his text *The Fifth Discipline: The Art & Practice of the Learning Organization*, writes that if our schools are alive and not static, if they are meant to meet the needs of learners, they need to be living systems guided by culture, climate, subsystems, structures, rituals, and routines that enable them to move and flow a certain way and heal. Self-healing mechanisms should be in place to ensure that anything that ruptures within that sense of safety, security, and trust will be repaired.

5

Restorative Practices for Repair and Healing

Our role as educators extends beyond the mere transmission of knowledge; it encompasses creating an environment that fosters emotional well-being, resilience, and holistic growth. Restorative practices have emerged as a potent tool within the realm of trauma-informed education, offering a comprehensive approach that addresses the intricate needs of students who have encountered trauma. There are multifaceted advantages of restorative practices as the preeminent form of trauma-based practice, elucidating their potential to empower students, cultivate relationships, facilitate emotional regulation, nurture essential life skills, and mitigate retraumatization.

Central to restorative practices is the principle of empowering students by endowing them with a voice in conflict resolution and decision-making processes. This empowerment assumes heightened significance for students who have undergone trauma, as it enables them to reclaim a sense of control and agency over their lives. By actively involving students in dialogues and decisions, restorative practices acknowledge their perspectives and engender mutual respect. Consequently, not only does this approach facilitate healing, but it also fosters a sense of ownership over one's actions and choices, marking a pivotal step toward repair and healing.

The aftermath of trauma often results in feelings of isolation and distrust, impeding the development of meaningful relationships. Restorative practices offer a space wherein students can forge connections with peers, educators, and the wider school community. Through mechanisms like restorative circles, cogenerative groups, personal narrative sharing, and group discussions, students are afforded opportunities to share their experiences, learn from their peers, and cultivate a sense of belonging. These interactions form a supportive network that aids the healing process and nurtures an atmosphere of holistic well-being. (*Cogenerative groups* are collaborative learning environments where students, teachers, and possibly other stakeholders come together to collectively analyze and improve educational practices. They aim to foster mutual learning and problem-solving by engaging participants in discussions, reflections, and actions to enhance teaching, learning, and the overall educational experience within a classroom or educational setting. More on them in Part D.)

Emotional dysregulation frequently ensues as a repercussion of trauma, rendering the management of feelings and responses a daunting endeavor. Restorative practices provide a structured platform through which students can articulate their emotions in a secure and constructive manner. By engaging in candid and open conversations, students acquire the tools to identify and express their emotions effectively. This newfound emotional regulation proves pivotal for trauma survivors, equipping them to navigate their emotions and responses more adeptly within and beyond the confines of the classroom.

Beyond the realm of conflict resolution, restorative practices bestow upon students vital life skills that extend far into their futures. Active listening, empathy, adept communication, and conflict resolution constitute the crux of restorative practices. These competencies not only amplify personal growth but also equip students with tools relevant to their academic and professional trajectories. By nurturing these proficiencies, restorative practices contribute to the comprehensive development of students, positioning them for success in various spheres of life.

Conventional punitive disciplinary measures, often perpetuating cycles of retraumatization, fall short in addressing the needs of students who have weathered significant trauma. Herein lies the differentiating strength of restorative practices, which prioritize understanding the root causes of behavior and providing support rather than punishment. This approach minimizes the risk of retraumatization and creates an environment of security and trust, where students are valued for their intrinsic worth rather than judged on their past experiences.

In essence, restorative practices represent an educational paradigm aligned seamlessly with the tenets of trauma-informed care. By empowering students, fostering relationships, facilitating emotional regulation, nurturing essential life skills, and mitigating retraumatization, restorative practices support trauma-based practice.

It is incumbent upon us, as educators, to not only acknowledge but also implement these practices, thereby creating an all-encompassing and nurturing educational culture and climate that recognizes and nurtures the potential for growth and healing inherent within every student, regardless of their past experiences. To delve into what this could look like in practice, let's return to Mirko and Pam's journey at the Putnam Avenue Upper School.

6

Righting a Sinking Ship With Restorative Practices

MIRKO CHARDIN

I first learned about restorative practices when I learned about restorative justice in South Africa, where I worked as a community organizer and the executive director of the New Hope Youth Coalition. I knew of the powerful work of restorative justice in the juvenile justice system and how there were circumstances where perpetrators and victims were brought together and dynamic healing took place. I was also familiar with the culture of restorative practices being implemented at the Boston Arts Academy; one of the founders was a mentor and former principal of mine, and this book's co-author Edgar Vasquez was at the helm of developing this culture. The school had mechanisms in place that allowed them to proactively identify, deal with, and mitigate conflict that erupted from student to student, student to teacher, teacher to student, and groups of students to teacher. And it was phenomenal. I wanted to learn more about their practices, so I spent time doing school visits and observations to determine what their systems and structures were and how they could work at my school.

I facilitated school visits and meetings where Pam, the founding assistant principal and also co-author of this text, and my counseling team engaged in conversations about restorative practices. We discussed them, we read articles, we did text-based discussions together, and we attended PD sessions on restorative practices to help develop our own understanding of it. While doing so, we struggled with how to bring this information back to the staff, because the ideas seemed so different from what they were used to, and it was hard to explain the concepts in ways that we thought made sense and didn't just sound theoretical. Then we landed on something. We realized the best way to teach about restorative practices was by ensuring the staff could experience them and then unpack what they were experiencing so that together we could create a sort of conceptual framework. Instead of inundating staff with research and data, we would simply share why we were considering these practices, provide some information about the school we were learning this concept from, and then have them experience restorative circles.

For our introduction to staff about restorative circles, we brought in Edgar, and this became the entry point of our journey together as school leaders and ultimately as the authors of this text. Pam and I reached out to Edgar due to what we learned about and saw firsthand during visits to his school. We consulted with him to learn about his school's journey and structures, and considering that we were learning with and from him, we thought it made sense to give our staff an opportunity to do the same.

Edgar facilitated a demo tier 1 (more on that soon) community-building circle, fishbowl-style, so that everyone could see what was happening. It was powerful. After a short mini-lesson, Edgar talked about the concepts and provided some PD and a historical framework of restorative practices. He then explained what we'd be doing and experiencing after we witnessed the fishbowl. The faculty members who were direct participants were debriefed in real time about what they had just experienced, publicly sharing their reflections and reactions. Those who observed as audience members then asked questions. Edgar was very clear that this was not just about disciplinary circumstances but about proactively implementing restorative practices in classrooms as a mechanism for capturing student voice and building community and trust. After the training, there was no immediate requirement or pressure on staff to utilize these practices. Our commitment was solely to explore and make sense of them and what they could look like if implemented at our school.

As a next step, we sought out faculty members who were willing to pilot restorative practices in their classrooms and allow colleagues to visit. The pilots went extremely well, and Pam and I made sure that we would always implement restorative practices when we responded to disciplinary circumstances. Being the chief disciplinarian and having trained in restorative practices via the International Institute of Restorative Practices as well as Suffolk University's Center for Restorative Justice, Pam became our point person to facilitate the training and capacity-building of other staff members. We also created opportunities for staff members to volunteer for training at Suffolk to formally learn about restorative practices.

The first folks willing to do pilots were two Grade 6 teachers and then it grew to the entire Grade 6 team. It was fascinating because teachers would just opt into applying restorative practices, and as this was happening, my assistant principal was also utilizing them more and more to navigate complex student conflicts with teachers. I was employing them as well, and a buzz was building. Teachers and kids alike were asking for restorative conferences and restorative circles.

Sometimes teachers struggling with classes would ask if Pam or I could facilitate a restorative circle to help them understand what was going on with their students. We had classes of students, even sixth graders, who requested that Pam, the counselors, or I come in and facilitate restorative circles because they didn't feel like class was going well and needed help to ensure that the teacher would listen to them. This organic flow led to us quickly scaling up restorative practices in our school community.

The next year we implemented circle practice at the seventh- and eighth-grade levels, and then we began the work of introducing it proactively through our advisory program. As we wrestled with social-emotional learning with our kiddos, we realized we could apply restorative practices in math classrooms to help us gauge whether or not our young people were actively engaged, whether or not they understood the learning objectives and targets, and whether or not they needed support.

We got to a place where restorative practices dynamically transformed the school community. Student voice was at the center. We embraced stories of self, developing our own public narratives in writing and sharing them among ourselves and then with our young people as we supported them in writing their own stories and sharing them as a school community; we invited in parents, caregivers, and others to participate in annual sharing and listening sessions. We completely shifted our data such that the Massachusetts Department of Secondary and Elementary Education lifted us up as an exemplar of not only restorative practices but cultural proficiency and representation as well. We had healed as a school community and were reaping the fruits. We had created a space that centered voice. We trusted each other, believed in each other, and believed in the kids and their caregivers. We experienced what John Hattie refers to as *collective teacher efficacy*, or the collective belief of teachers in their ability to positively affect students (Visible Learning, 2018), and it moved the needle for us in dynamic ways.

We also realized that this wasn't just about the faculty, staff, and students; it was about parents, caregivers, and community members as well, so we created systems and structures that involved their voices, too. We created a quarterly event known as Community Conversations, a space where adults in the community could learn and hear the voices of parents and caregivers. We restructured our school council meetings to ensure that school council members participated in the same professional learning that teachers wrestled with so that they could share their feedback on what they thought worked or didn't work.

We truly understood that voice has to be at the center, and that it's a scary thing but an authentic thing, and it leads to dynamic success. We embraced the notions that all means all—all have voices, and all voices matter—and that hearing does not necessarily mean agreeing with each other all the time but listening, learning from, reflecting, and valuing each other. Through a culture of intentional universally designed restorative practices, we healed and became a healthy and thriving school community.

As we continue on our journey through this text, you'll learn that our experiences with healing through restorative practices were not unique. There is an Indigenous context to these practices that reinforces their roots and effectiveness, and educators and practitioners across the globe have also experienced healing and success when they implement restorative practices appropriately as a mechanism to gather and hear voice. Please keep reading to learn more.

7

Pause and Reflect On Part A

SUMMARY

Part A prompts us to address a crucial need: healing our school cultures. The stories we've explored remind us of the trauma lurking in our education system. In today's world, the call for healing school cultures is more pressing than ever. Ongoing societal upheaval, like the COVID-19 pandemic and divisive forces, has left our educational landscape uncertain. Still, schools have the potential to heal if we approach them with intent. Healing involves ensuring equitable access and rethinking systems, structures, and routines. It means addressing elements of a white supremacy culture and bridging the gap between individualism and collectivism. Healing ensures that unheard voices are heard, new perspectives explored, and power dynamics reshaped.

Restorative practices play a vital role in this transformation, promoting connections, emotional regulation, and essential life skills. As we work together to mend our school cultures, educators take on the role of healers, aiming to provide a nurturing space for every student, regardless of their past. Our journey includes exploring restorative practices and engaging in reflective conversations to foster acceptance, empowerment, and progress.

For the next steps, we hope to support you as you commit to learning more about restorative practices and how they can positively impact your school culture. As you continue reading this text, we encourage you to explore the reflective questions at the end of each chapter, either through journaling or by having courageous conversations with colleagues.

REFLECTION QUESTIONS

1. Can you recall instances from your own educational experiences that mirror the discomfort and exclusion described in the vignettes at the beginning of the chapter?

2. How has recent global upheaval, including the pandemic and societal divisions, impacted your perception of school culture and its role in students' lives?

3. In what ways can your educational community embrace equitable access and inclusive practices to foster a healing school culture? As an educator, how can you actively contribute to the creation of a safe, empowering, and healing environment for all learners?

4. Have you encountered restorative practices in your educational journey? How might these practices contribute to healing and growth within your school community?

5. Reflecting on your role as an educator, how might you integrate the principles of trauma-informed care into your approach to teaching and interacting with students?

PART B

Restorative Practices, Indigenous Origins

Healing begins where the wound was made.
—Alice Walker,
African American novelist and activist

8

It Started Over Pancakes

PAM CHU-SHERIFF

My three-year-old daughter is obsessed with pancakes. Ever since my husband started making her pancakes from scratch, that's all she ever wants to eat. Mind you, she has a fairly extensive vocabulary for a three-year-old, but anytime you ask her what she wants for breakfast, the answer is "pancakes." When she plays with her stuffed animals and pretends to feed them, what is her Rilakkuma stuffed animal pretending to eat? Pancakes. What is she pretending to go grocery shopping for? Yes, pancakes.

Apparently, middle school boys are also obsessed with pancakes. When it came time for the eighth grade to get ready for their MCAS tests, the state standardized test in Massachusetts, our eighth-grade teachers graciously offered to cook breakfast for all of the students on the morning of the first day of testing. I distinctly remember on my morning rounds that day how the sweet, comforting smell of pancakes coming from Room 312 wafted through the hallways. I popped my head into the room and saw one of the teachers pouring batter onto a griddle that she had hauled into her classroom all the way from home, and she was soon busy flipping pancakes and pouring syrup for students in her morning advisory. I walked downstairs to my office with a warm and fuzzy feeling inside, grateful for a calm and caring start to the morning, and for the camaraderie evident among our students and staff.

I had gotten seated at my desk when I got an urgent call from the front desk. There had been a physical altercation in Room 312. More specifically, one student, Kelvin, had "dropped" another student, Martin (both are pseudonyms). And for those who need a translation, to "drop" someone means to hoist them in the air, WWE-style, and smash them to the ground. I rushed back upstairs with a very different feeling in the pit of my stomach.

As it turns out, the fight started when Martin had tried to enter Kelvin's advisory to get in on the pancake action. Kelvin was having no part of any pancake party crashers, so he dutifully blocked the doorway. Undeterred, Martin continued to try to push his way into the classroom. Soon enough, a scuffle broke out between the two students, culminating in Kelvin picking up Martin and smashing him to the floor. Thankfully, Martin did not have any physical injuries, but there was no question that great harm had been caused not only between Kelvin and Martin but also within Kelvin's advisory. The entire class had witnessed the incident, and the general consensus was, *Really? Over* pancakes?

Once he had calmed down, Kelvin was mortified about what had happened and terrified about the impending phone call home. Kelvin was given a serious consequence due to instigating a physical altercation. As can be wonderfully confounding about middle schoolers, Kelvin and Martin were hanging out with each other after school shortly after the incident, their friendship apparently unaffected (I held a restorative conference between the two, though, just in case. More on those later!). What I was most concerned about was what things would be like for Kelvin when he returned to his advisory. Kelvin's classmates were not fine with him.

Kelvin himself knew that his classmates were talking smack about him. I told him that we—as in Kelvin, his class, the teacher, and I—needed to address what had happened and talk about it as a group via a restorative circle. He knew that I had run circles in other classes, and after I role-played with him and reviewed what he wanted to say, he agreed, albeit nervously, to hold a circle with his peers. Before holding the circle, I checked in with the teacher to schedule a time, shared the circle agenda and questions with her for feedback, and asked her to prep her students for the discussion.

The morning of the circle, a simple Do Now was projected on the board. "Welcome! Grab a seat in the circle." The goals were twofold but simple: Reflect on last week's incident and reflect on how to move forward. I had chosen a cute monster stuffed animal for our talking piece, as that seemed to be popular with students whenever they saw it in my office. We started the circle with our usual practice: an opener. I asked students to reflect on the quote, "Forget the mistake, remember the lesson." I asked everyone to silently meditate upon what that might mean and why I had chosen it to begin our discussion. Before diving into more serious talk, everyone went around and shared their responses to a low-stakes prompt, "Name someone you look up to." Students started to open up, and walls started to come down as they shared some personal examples (someone shared that they considered their grandfather their best friend) and some controversial ones (Kyrie Irving elicited a few groans). The meat and potatoes of the circle were our two discussion rounds, which were: What was going through your mind during and after Thursday's incident? What would you like to say to the class/student in terms of moving forward?

Both Kelvin and his classmates were profoundly honest, articulate, and respectful. Classmates who had been laughing at how Kelvin had lost his temper were giving him sage advice on what to do next time and offered to support him if he ever felt like he was going to lose his cool again. Kelvin, for his part, took in the words from his peers better than any advice an adult could have given him. And in a pleasant twist, Kelvin gave a heartfelt apology to his classmates for his behavior. Although Kelvin and I had previously role-played what he and his classmates might say during this time, he had told me that, even though he regretted his behavior, he didn't feel comfortable apologizing, mostly because he felt too embarrassed to. In no way was I going to force him to (a forced apology isn't much of an apology!), but in the moment, he felt compelled to really let his peers know that he had completely crossed a line and wanted to make things right. We closed out the circle by reflecting again on the quote that we had opened with, "Forget the mistake, remember the lesson," and the words seemed to have even more resonance the second time around. As the advisory block ended, several students nonchalantly dapped Kelvin up, and the class was slowly dismissed and trickled into the hallway. It seemed that, for now at least, all was right again in the world of Room 312's advisory.

Now let's step back and consider if the situation between Kelvin and Martin had occurred in a traditional school setting. Most likely Kelvin and Martin would have received a consequence for being involved in a physical altercation, and their parents would have been notified. Some schools might have offered a mediation for the two students, and from there, it's usually case closed. All too often when a conflict has occurred and harm has been caused, the end goal is the consequence, and very little consideration goes into taking into account the needs of *all* of those who have been affected by one person's actions. While consequences can be necessary, modified, or replaced with restorative measures depending on the incident, these accountability measures cannot be at the expense of considering how to factor in opportunities for healing. Let's say Kelvin had not participated in the restorative circle with his classmates even though he had broken the trust of his community. His return to advisory would surely have filled him with anxiety or dread, possibly resulting in him shutting down or perhaps continuing to act out. Some of his classmates would have shunned or mocked him. The classroom climate would have been menacing at worst and awkward at best—hardly conditions conducive to learning or feeling a sense of community.

9

What Are Restorative Practices?

In the education world, you may have heard terms like *circle practice*, *restorative practice*, or *restorative justice*. What exactly are these, do they matter, should you be using them in your learning environments, and what do they mean for student discipline and for school climate and culture? We've set out to clarify the terminology and help you understand how using restorative practices in your schools and classrooms can help build more equity in your learning environments.

Restorative practices are a framework and range of approaches that aim to develop community and relationships and to prevent and repair conflict and harm. In short, they are intentional practices that restore agency in ways that treat humans with dignity and respect. Circle practice, one of the more formalized restorative practices approaches, is a structured, egalitarian group process in which participants sit in a circle and take turns responding to discussion prompts. The purposes of circles can vary widely, from simply building community to addressing conflict or harm.

On the other hand, restorative justice is a subset of restorative practices and aims to hold offenders accountable for their wrongs by involving them in repair processes with the people they have harmed. As stated earlier, while *restorative practices* and *restorative justice* are often used interchangeably, in this book we use the term *restorative practices* since restorative justice has close ties to the criminal justice system. Words matter, and the last thing we want to do is to contribute to the criminalization of our young people. At the same time, this choice is by no means meant to shame or shade any school programs that currently use the term *restorative justice*.

Restorative practices are often hailed as an alternative to traditional measures, which frequently hold an individual accountable through punitive consequences without ensuring closure. Restorative practices have increasingly been adopted for usage in schools as a potential alternative to punitive consequences and out-of-school suspensions. While many schools have had success employing restorative practices, many others have struggled to succeed. Perhaps this is because they have missed the fact that the foundational elements of the practice and purpose are rooted in a cultural schema of collectivism, are a part of many Indigenous cultures, and are structured within this context as a means of extending, protecting, and honoring cultural values and norms through the communal experience of speaking your truth and listening to others speak theirs.

As Barbara Sherrod describes in Dr. Edward C. Valandra's seminal text *Colorizing Restorative Justice: Voicing Our Realities*, "Restorative practices have been around for centuries, but Western modernity has reduced them to nothing more than an alternative to a punitive system" (Valandra, 2020, p. 56). Restorative practices should be seen not as a quick fix but rather as a full-scale paradigm shift in how we view our students, relationships, and school culture. We must remember that the firm goal of restorative practices is to develop community and relationships and to prevent and repair conflict and harm. This is not simply about implementing a tool during challenging times to magically resolve conflict. Instead, it is a framework that communicates a message: If we can trust each other with our voices because we know that they will be heard, and if we commit to also respecting and listening to the voices and experiences of others, then we can build better communities where all learners feel a sense of belonging. This can be incredibly powerful when woven into the fabric of classroom and school culture.

A RANGE OF APPROACHES

The notion of restorative practices may seem new to you, but ask yourself whether you have ever engaged in any of the following activities:

- Expressed to a young person how their actions made you feel (e.g., "I'm so proud of you for . . . !," "I was really disappointed when . . .").

- Asked a young person how something impacted them, either negatively or positively.

- Asked a young person to think about the impact of their actions after they were involved in some type of conflict.

- Seen two young people get into a conflict with each other, pulled them aside, asked them what happened, and helped them to discuss the situation and apologize to each other.

- Sat in a circle with a group of people and had everyone go around and respond to a check-in question.

- Held a meeting between students or between a student and a staff member to work to resolve an incident that occurred between them.

If you answered yes to any of the questions above, then you have already experienced some type of restorative practice.

Restorative practices can be thought of as falling along a continuum ranging from informal to formal (Wachtel, 2016), as shown in Figure B-1. It includes strategies like simply being mindful of the way we speak, encouraging others to reflect, and holding structured meetings.

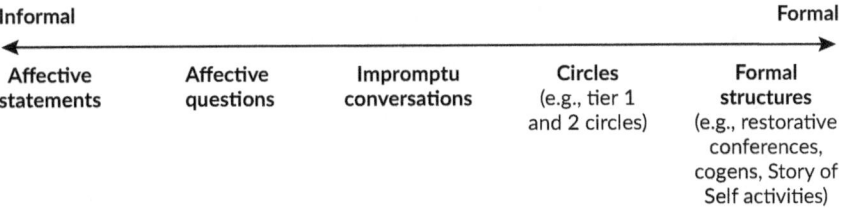

FIGURE B-1: The restorative practices continuum (adapted from Ted Wachtel's Restorative Practices Continuum, 2016)

Beginning with the most informal approaches, *affective statements* are statements in which we express our emotions, feelings, or attitudes about personal reactions or sentiments toward a situation, event, or experience. These would be akin to saying to a student, "I'm so proud of you for participating in the discussion today," or, "I was really disappointed to hear that you were teasing your classmate."

Next, *affective questions* inquire about emotions, feelings, or attitudes, aiming to explore or understand someone's emotional state, perspective, or reactions. This could be asking a student, "How do you think that made her feel when you made a negative post about her on Instagram? How would you feel if someone did that to you?"

Impromptu conversations are unplanned or spontaneous conversations in which individuals convene to discuss and address immediate or emerging issues, often without prior preparation or formal scheduling. Ask any teacher who's been on lunch or recess duty recently, and they're sure to have a story of, say, pulling apart two students who got into a tiff, facilitating a conversation where the students talk it out, and then having the students resolve to move on and do better next time.

Again, many of these statements, questions, or spontaneous conversations are teaching moves that come to educators organically, but it is important to recognize that even the day-to-day language we use is a crucial part of creating a climate that values reflection and perspective taking.

10

Circle Practice

Moving into the realm of more formal approaches, *circles* are next on the continuum. As these are often the bedrock of creating a restorative climate, we'll take some time to explore them in depth and to discuss the mechanics of running circles.

As kindergarteners, we might have been made to sit in circles for reading time, share-out time, math time, and the like. While we were sitting in circles, there were no large pieces of furniture obstructing our views of each other. During circle time, we might have felt connected, heard, seen, and acknowledged. Everyone had a chance to share out while the rest of the group listened. Circles have always been present and alive in education. They exemplify a space where everyone is on a level playing field and feels safe and welcome.

Circles are a whole-group, inclusive approach that fosters a sense of community because everyone participates in discussions that either address general topics and issues or focus on specific concerns. A community-building circle could be as simple as a regular check-in during homeroom: Students are seated (or standing) in a circle and take turns to share, say, a highlight from their weekend, their goal for the week, or what their desired superpower would be and why. A repair circle, on the other hand, would be held in response to a specific incident or situation, such as the circle that was held with Kelvin and his advisory.

Circle practice can be transformative and is a powerful tool for fostering and strengthening students' social-emotional competencies of self-management, social awareness, relationship skills, self-awareness, and responsible decision-making. Oftentimes, achieving the desired outcome of a circle all comes down to planning. Key elements to consider when designing circles include the following:

1. **Goal:** What is my purpose in running this circle?
2. **Opening:** How will I open the circle—a poem, quote, song, breathing, story, or something else?
3. **Introduction of talking piece:** What object am I using, and why?
4. **Check-in:** What question will I ask?
5. **Guidelines/values:** What questions will I ask to create shared guidelines and values?
6. **Discussion rounds:** What needs to be addressed in the circle? What questions will I ask? How many rounds?
7. **Check-out:** How are people feeling right now?
8. **Closing:** How will I close this circle—a poem, quote, song, breathing, story, or something else?

As the name implies, participants should be seated in their chairs in circle formation, ideally with no tables or other furniture positioned between the participants (students can also form a circle on the floor or sit on their desks in circle formation). The circle represents "shared leadership, equality, connection, and inclusion" (Pranis, 2005). The circle might include a centerpiece displaying the group's shared values or other ceremonial elements of significance to the group. The centerpiece also provides a place for participants to rest their eyes. The facilitator, or circle keeper, maintains the collective space by encouraging participants to share openly and honestly, posing the discussion questions, and reminding participants of the group's shared values as necessary.

The *talking piece* is an object used to regulate communication by letting people know whose turn it is to talk while everyone else listens. Only the person who has the talking piece can speak, a practice that encourages respectful listening and models the importance of every voice. Both talking and listening are important; mutual understanding lays the groundwork for deeper, more meaningful connection, reflection, and discussion. Receiving the talking piece is an invitation to share with the group and helps ensure that everyone gets an opportunity to share at their own pace and in their own way without interruptions. Individuals can share what they want, remain silent during their turn, or pass by giving the talking piece to the next person. As the talking piece is passed around the circle, each participant has a turn to share their authentic personal stories and have them respectfully heard and acknowledged without shame, blame, or judgment.

As you establish guidelines and values, keep in mind that it is even more powerful to create them together or, at the very least, to get input or agreement on them. These four guidelines are a great starting place, and of course, can be modified depending on participant input and needs:

1. Respect the talking piece.

2. Speak from and listen with your heart.

3. Speak and listen with respect.

4. Honor confidentiality.

Use Table B-1 to guide you through the circle planning process. Remember, you don't have to cover all of these steps each time you hold a circle. It all depends on the amount of time, frequency, and purpose of your circle(s), as well as the participants' familiarity with the process.

TABLE B-1: Circle Planning Template

1. Goal	
2. Opening	
3. Talking piece	
4. Check-in	
5. Guidelines/values	
6. Discussion rounds	
7. Check-out	
8. Closing	

TIPS FOR RUNNING CIRCLES

Circles Take Trust

One of the most powerful things about circles is that they give a voice to the voiceless. All too often, student voices are set on the back burner, if they even have a place at all. With circles, students have the opportunity to develop a sense of agency and to feel empowered. However, in order for students to feel comfortable enough to share candidly, they must develop a sense of trust not only with their peers but also with the adult running the circle. An essential factor in our success with running circles across all of our schools has been the strong relationships we've built with our students.

Let's say you want to run a more targeted repair circle with a class that has become somewhat toxic. The teacher is ready to listen to some hard feedback, and the students pretty much think that there's nowhere to go but up from here. In the discovery phase, so to speak, of gathering information before actually holding the circle, it's important to schedule a time to speak to some of those high-leverage students with that all-too-important social capital and influence to see what's going on. If that trust isn't there, students will inevitably see you as just another authority figure and will not authentically open up to you or the process.

Circles Take Willingness

When we share examples of circles in which students openly discussed some pretty weighty issues and arrived at realistic solutions, or when we mention how staff members took ownership over their own mistakes in front of a classroom full of students, the reaction can sometimes be one of incredulity. Yet it's important to remember that one of the keys to a productive circle is a willingness on the part of all parties to engage in an honest, respectful dialogue. More specifically, willingness on the part of the adults to be open to critical feedback and to make changes in their practice is absolutely crucial. Let's revisit the example of holding a circle to address a toxic classroom environment. If the teacher scoffs at the idea of listening to student feedback and taking ownership over their own mistakes, there's no way that the circle can be successful. In fact, the repair circle should not even take place.

Circles Take Work

Perhaps surprisingly, one of the biggest obstacles to successfully implementing circles is simply all of the planning and logistics involved. For instance, staff might want to set aside part of their class period for community-building circles, but carving out time against competing interests can often be difficult. Or consider how, to the untrained eye, a seamless community-building circle may look like a simple icebreaker activity. However, those who have implemented circles with fidelity are all too familiar with the hard work involved in establishing norms, building a positive classroom culture, and deciding on the appropriate prompts and circle activities that best meet the needs of their particular cohort of students.

When scheduling more targeted harm or repair circles, it is sometimes a Herculean task to find a day and time that works for everyone—the students, staff, facilitator, and family members (as necessary). There's also all of the planning that goes into creating discussion-round questions, which may also be done in conjunction with the teacher or student(s), as well as the meetings that must be held with certain students before the circle to gauge what might be expected and what students might say. What's more, if the circle ends up being scheduled too far down the line, it might lose its connection to, and therefore its impact on, the event or events that triggered the circle in the first place. In short, though, if we truly value the restorative nature of circles, we must prove it by putting in the work to make them happen.

Circles Take Time

Let's go back to the example of a repair circle to address a toxic classroom. Say you've wrapped it up, the students and the teacher all respectfully and honestly shared what was going on, and the group collectively came up with some next steps for moving forward. All of the participants should be reminded that, say, a 45-minute discussion is not going to suddenly change or solve things overnight. It is simply the first—not the last—step in a cooperative, ongoing process. And this process needs time to play itself out, to allow space for minor setbacks, and to give students and staff opportunities to regroup and make progress. This is also why it's important to schedule follow-up circles as a means of monitoring progress.

11

Formal Structures

After circles, at the farthest end of the restorative practices continuum are *formal structures*, which typically involve individualized, intensive meetings or interventions tailored to specific students who require significant support or specialized attention due to academic, behavioral, or social-emotional challenges. These conferences can involve a multidisciplinary team and focus on developing highly personalized strategies to address the student's needs.

As part of the restorative practices toolkit at our own school site, we also employed *cogenerative dialogues*, or cogens, which Dr. Christopher Emdin describes as structured conversations "between the teacher and their students with a goal of co-creating/generating plans of action for improving the classroom" (2016, p. 66). We will explore cogens in more depth in Part C.

Lastly, because honoring our identities is an essential part of cultivating a sense of belonging, as administrators at the Putnam Avenue Upper School, we engaged our entire school community—staff and students—in various Story of Self activities, which were inspired by Marshall Ganz's research around public narratives. Ganz, a long-time community organizer and professor at Harvard University's Kennedy School of Government, describes how writing a "story of self," using the framework of identifying a challenge, a choice, and an outcome, not only enables us to be mindful of our own decisions and experiences but also, when these stories are shared within a community, the collective wisdom and experience can be a motivating factor for all (2009). Engaging our students and staff in these activities created a shared sense of purpose and will be explored in more detail in Part C. Due to the structured, communal nature of Story of Self activities, these can also be considered one of many formal structures that can be utilized to incorporate more restorative practices into school settings.

In addition to the continuum, we can also conceptualize restorative practices as multitiered in nature (see Figure B-2, adapted from Morrison, 2005):

- Tier 1 approaches are *universal* in that they are proactive and center on reaffirming relationships through building social and emotional skills. In schools, this might look like daily, weekly, or monthly tier 1 circles focused on community building. These can be held anywhere from advisories and town halls or in core academic classes and specialty classes.

- Tier 2 practices are *targeted* and focus on repairing relationships in classrooms or groups. It is important to designate trained staff or create a restorative practices (RP) team that is responsible for facilitating tier 2 circles. This might be work shared among school administrators, school counselors, and social workers. Some schools are fortunate enough to have the funds for designated RP staff or part-time specialists who can also facilitate this work. The restorative circle held with Kelvin and his advisory class after he got into a physical altercation is an example of a tier 2 practice.

- Tier 3 approaches are *intensive* and center on rebuilding relationships via conferencing and mediation. Each school should have its own process for deciding when a tier 3 conference or reentry meeting should be held. The school's RP team should be able to recommend tier 3 restorative conferences or wrap-around reentry meetings and should also have the capacity to field requests for these interventions from staff, students, or families.

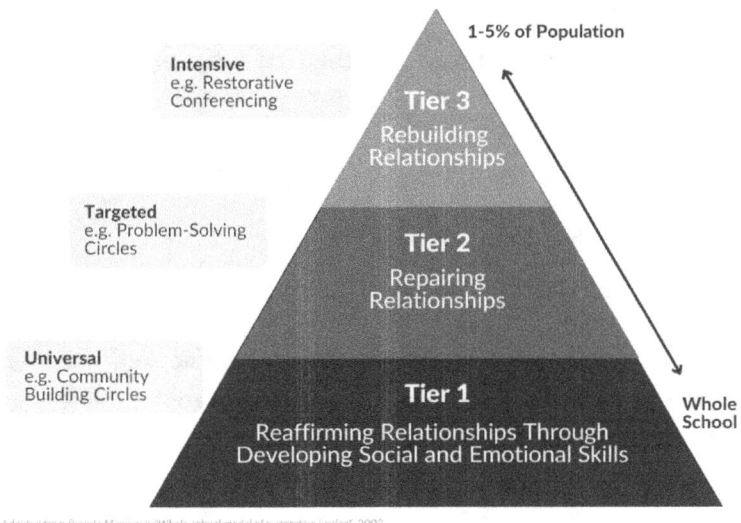

FIGURE B-2: Whole-school model of restorative practices (adapted from Morrison, 2005)

The following list of restorative questions can form the basis of tier 2 and tier 3 restorative circles and conferences (again, it is worth noting that facilitating tier 2 and 3 practices requires additional training and experience; many schools designate particular staff, such as administrators, counselors, or teachers who have received additional training to be responsible for these practices). The questions can be adapted depending on each situation, but it is vital to ensure that whatever the wording, the discussion should be based in having participants voice what they were thinking at the time of the incident, what they have learned since the incident, and what needs to be done to move forward. One tip when using these restorative questions: If participants are asked to share about what happened, the facilitator must make clear that the point of the conversation is not to debate the ins and outs of what occurred and not to get mired in the details of what transpired; the goal is to reflect on what lessons have been learned and what needs to be done to move forward.

Restorative questions for tier 2 and 3 circles (adapted from White, 2012):

1. What happened, and what were you thinking at the time?

2. What have you thought about since?

3. Who has been affected by what happened and how?

4. What about this has been the hardest for you?

5. What do you think needs to be done to make things right?

As with many tiered models, the more we can proactively frontload our time and efforts into strengthening our tier 1 practices, the less we will need to reactively provide targeted or intensive tier 2 and 3 supports.

12

The Social Discipline Window

Take a moment and think back to when you were a kid. Did you ever have a coach or caregiver who was super-strict, the "my way or the highway" type? If so, how did you or other young people respond to that style? Perhaps you obeyed out of fear, but perhaps you also craved some encouragement and kind words every now and then. Or picture that teacher who always wants to be friends with their students. Maybe they're the cool teacher who kids love, but sometimes boundaries are unclear, and a culture of permissiveness reigns. Unfortunately, we've also probably all seen or heard of examples of parents or caregivers who, for whatever reason, are not able to be very present in their children's lives. Discipline and a nurturing environment are both absent, and this type of neglect can lead to disastrous results for the whole family.

On the flip side, that sweet spot in which we offer both clear boundaries and ample encouragement results in young people who have clear guidance, learn to understand limits, and can build a connection with that adult. These varying styles illustrate the *social discipline window*, which describes how those in positions of authority can approach interactions with young people (Wachtel, 2016). As Figure B-3 illustrates, one axis is control, which includes setting boundaries and limits. The other axis is support, which entails providing a nurturing environment. Both control and support are needed; we cannot have just one or the other. If there's only high control, we become like that overbearing, authoritative coach or parent. If there's only high support, we're that teacher who lets anything slide in order to be friends with their students. If we have neither, we are neglectful. When we can provide our young people with both discipline and love, they will know that we are with them on this journey.

Wachtel and McCold (2004) state, "Human beings are happier, more cooperative and productive, and more likely to make positive changes in their behavior when those in positions of authority do things with them, rather than to them or for them." (para. 2) This restorative approach to interacting gives students a sense of agency while also allowing them to build a relationship with a trusted adult.

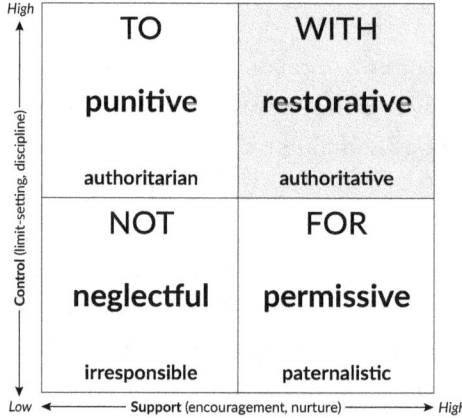

FIGURE B-3: The social discipline window (adapted from Wachtel, 2016)

13

Indigenous Origins

While we describe restorative practices and restorative justice as movements or fields, it is important to acknowledge that those descriptors are born of a Western, colonial lens. Restorative practices are rooted in various Indigenous cultures and communities around the world that have traditionally engaged in communal healing and listening cycles as a means to celebrate, teach, respect, and honor each other. We must not only honor these origins but also recognize that there is great diversity among various Indigenous justice systems and beliefs.

The Maori of New Zealand, for instance, have a deep cultural history rooted in community and restoration; conflicts were not the responsibility of individuals but rather involved a larger system of the offender, the victim, and the families of both (Pratt, 1996). Before punitive, colonial laws were forced upon the Maori with the brutal wave of British colonization in the 1800s, the Maori concept of justice was built on the notion that any harmful behavior (*hara*) was due to "an imbalance to the social equilibrium" (p. 138). More specifically:

> *Conflict resolution took the form of a hearing held on the marae (area in front of the communal meeting house, or wharaenui) or inside a special wharenui called the wharerunanga. Its purpose was to investigate the matter and attempt to restore*

> the balance that had been disturbed, usually by redressing the harm done to the victim. The quantity of redress would be dependent on the degree of the offense: a form of compensation (utu) for some, with mediation to remove causes of tension ... the interests of the victim and his or her family or tribe were central to the administration of justice. (pp. 138–139)

Here we see a holistic, communal approach that focuses on restoration and addressing harm rather than strictly focusing on consequences.

Similarly, the traditional Navajo judicial system was built upon the notion of restoring harmony rather than on punitive measures (Meyer, 1998). If an individual violated a community norm, that individual would be subject to a system rooted in clan relations and mediation (1998). This relational structure is so deeply embedded in the Navajo belief systems that it is said of a wrongdoer, "He acts as if he had no relatives" (Yazzie & Zion, 1996, p. 162). However, these justice systems began to take on different forms as European colonization imposed their own systems of courts and laws upon Indigenous peoples (Meyer, 1998). However, in 1982, judges from the Navajo Nation were able to revive and institutionalize their traditional system of justice, or *hozhooji naat"aanii*, which roughly translates to "peacemaking" in English (Zion, 1998). Today, the Navajo Nation's court system still centers on peacemaking and is considered the largest tribal legal system in the world (Austin & Williams, 2009).

As Navajo Nation Chief Justice Emeritus Robert Yazzie and native studies scholar James Zion write, "Navajo justice methods are corrective in the sense that they attempt to get at causes that underlie disputes or wrongdoing" (1996, p. 171). Navajo corrective justice, they continue,

> is not so much concerned about correction of the person as it is about restoring that person to good relations with others ... another function of Navajo justice is known as distributive justice. Where there is an injury, the group identifies resources to address it.... Distributive justice asks, "what do we have and how can we help?" (p. 172)

While it is important to honor the Indigenous historical roots of present-day restorative practices, it is equally crucial to note that there are current Native practices and voices that we can continue to lift up and learn from.

Restorative practices and restorative justice also have deep roots in various African countries, where they existed long before European colonization. For instance, the Kinga people of southern Tanzania resolved conflict by using restorative justice processes (Gabagambi, 2020). If an issue arose within or among clans, a reconciliation meeting was held. Members of the community would gather in a type of court setting known as *Lugono*. As participants sat in a circle around a fireplace, a complainant would describe the incident, and the defendant or defendants would respond. The parties would commemorate their reconciliation by sharing from the same pot of alcohol, known as *ukupelanila ulupelo*, and eating roasted meat, or *okukatelanila inyama*, together (2020).

Similarly, many communities in Nigeria have also long practiced restorative justice (Gabagambi, 2020). After mediating a dispute, councils of elders would ensure genuine reconciliation by having both parties eat from the same bowl. This could include drinking palm wine, *burukutu* (a popular alcoholic beverage made from sorghum grains and fermented guinea corn), or local gin from the same cup; participants might also break and eat kola nuts together (2020).

Circle practice, also known as talking circles, peacemaking circles, or healing circles, is deeply rooted in the practices of Indigenous people, including the First Nations people of Canada (Mehl-Madrona & Mainguy, 2014). Jean Stevenson (1999), Cree of Peguis First Nation, Manitoba, describes how the circle is a sacred symbol of life's interdependence as well as a key symbol in Native spirituality and family life: "We dance in circles, our Drums are round, the Sweat lodge is round, the Tipi is round, and the Medicine Wheel is round" (p. 9). In healing circles, participants share their journeys and difficulties and can learn from and draw closer to one another in the process. Healing circles are being increasingly used today with both native and non-native communities in Canada to provide support for issues from addiction and violence to grief and trauma (1999).

In addition, many Indigenous cultures used talking sticks as a means for a group to speak in turn and also as symbols of power. Dr. Carol Locust, Eastern Band Cherokee, describes their use:

> *The Talking Stick has been used for centuries by many tribes as a means of just and impartial hearing. The Talking Stick was commonly used in council circles to decide who had the right to speak. When matters of great concern would come before the council, the leading elder would hold the Talking Stick, and begin the discussion. When he would finish what he had to say, he would hold out the Talking Stick and whoever would speak after him would take it. In this manner, the stick would be passed from one individual to another until all who wanted to speak had done so. The stick then was passed back to the elder for safe keeping.* (Tavares Avant, 2018, para. 7)

For the Akan people of West Africa, *Ōkyeame poma*, or staffs of office, were used by "the highest ranking member of the royal or chiefly entourage in the Akan court system" (Windmuller-Luna, 2015, para. 7). These individuals were gifted public speakers whose primary role was to mediate the chief's speech, and they eventually became mediators between clan groups (2015). The Maori *tokotoko*, or orator's staff, is an ornate, ceremonial staff, usually carried by males, that signifies that the holder is skilled in the arts of *whaikōrero* (formal speeches), *karakia* (prayer), and storytelling (Museum of New Zealand, n.d.).

THE FIRST HARM

While restorative practices owes its roots to a variety of Indigenous peoples from around the world, it is also clear that European colonization, with its forced imposition of a different set of justice systems and laws, has in some cases eroded or completely decimated these traditional justice processes. However, Indigenous restorative frameworks and approaches are seeing revitalization and renewed interest in countries around the world, whether it be in court systems or in education systems. Thus, as new or seasoned practitioners today, we must be careful to not repeat these same cycles of colonization by—sometimes unwittingly—claiming these practices as our own and turning them into tools of control and oppression.

Dr. Edward C. Valandra, Waŋbli Waphåha Hokšíla, a Native American scholar raised on the Rosebud Sioux Reservation, writes extensively of what he refers to as the "First Harm." He states, "The US was birthed with genocide and slavery," and "the legacies of these massive harms remain enforced today" (2020, p. 29). Thus, we must return to where the wound was made so that healing can begin. He writes of how restorative practices go hand in hand with issues of race and justice: "Siloing RJ [restorative justice] from racial and social justice issues, including de/colonization—as if RJ/RP could be effective, much less fulfill its promise and potential, in a 'color blind,' injustice blind bubble—is not an option" (p. 31). If we ignore systemic inequality, we risk co-opting and colonizing a practice that we purport to be honoring, and we risk perpetuating the same cycles of exploitation that have repeatedly harmed already marginalized communities.

Dr. Gaye Lang describes an unfortunate reality in which "the restorative community has itself normalized racial behavior antithetical to RJ/RP values" and "identifies what ails restorative practices: the Western world, and co-opting and institutionalizing circles, has done so within the framework of white supremacy" (Valandra, 2020, p. 12). She advises that we must first name and challenge this paradigm in order to dismantle it.

Sharon Goens-Bradley, a restorative practices practitioner and woman of color, advises that in order to authentically engage in the work of restorative practices, circle keepers must "cultivate cross-cultural competence," which includes the following:

- Learning about their own and others social identities, especially around race, culture, religious beliefs, and lived experiences

- Identifying their own unconscious biases and learning specific strategies and supports for interrupting them in real time

- Learning how to build cross-cultural relationships and how to engage in respectful (even if uncomfortable) cross-cultural conflict

- Building the capacity to hear and respond to honest feedback related to race, racism, and racial privilege without personalizing the feedback

- Learning about the systemic privilege and power attached to specific identities in the United States and learning strategies for evening the playing field within specific individual and group interactions

- Engaging in ongoing individual and group work to understand all the ways in which racism manifests internally, personally, and systemically (for those circle keepers who are White, this includes learning to speak and listen with greater humility and accountability)

- Learning how to engage cross-culturally with empathy and, specifically, looking at issues through others' worldviews (Valandra, 2020, p. 48)

Developing these competencies is a lifelong process that, while difficult, is absolutely necessary. One of the best ways to honor these Indigenous traditions and histories is to ensure that our present-day implementation of restorative practices centers on justice. In order to truly carry out restorative practices with fidelity, we cannot ignore issues of equity. We cannot tiptoe around or sidestep altogether difficult conversations around race, racism, and injustice. As adults and practitioners, if we cannot model this vulnerability, discomfort, and ongoing learning and listening process for our young people, how can we expect them to do the same?

14

Restorative Practices in Schools

Beginning in the 1980s, school discipline was heavily characterized by a zero-tolerance approach, punitive measures, and exclusionary discipline practices such as suspensions and expulsions (Marsh, 2017). According to Marsh, President Clinton's passing of the Gun-Free Schools Act in 1994 and the Columbine High School mass shooting in 1999 served to bolster these zero-tolerance policies across the nation. As Marsh describes, "the growing prevalence of surveillance in the forms of cameras, metal detectors, drug-sniffing dogs, security-oriented School Resource Officers, and police on school grounds" (p. 2) became further symbols of students being treated as criminals. Perhaps not surprisingly, the rates of suspensions and expulsions became "remarkably high," with 3.5 million students suspended in school, 3.45 million suspended out of school, and 130,000 expelled during the 2011–12 school year (U.S. Department of Education Office for Civil Rights, 2014) out of the 49 million students enrolled in U.S. schools.

Perhaps even more unsurprisingly, the disproportionate rates at which students of color faced punitive, disciplinary measures versus their White counterparts became strikingly clear. In a landmark 2014 data snapshot on school discipline, the U.S. Department of Education Office for Civil Rights found the following:

- **Disproportionately high suspension/expulsion rates for students of color:** Black students are suspended and expelled at a rate three times greater than White students. On average, 5% of White students are suspended compared to 16% of Black students. American Indian and Native Alaskan students are also disproportionately suspended and expelled, representing less than 1% of the student population but 2% of out-of-school suspensions and 3% of expulsions.

- **Disproportionate suspensions of girls of color:** While boys receive more than two out of three suspensions, Black girls are suspended at higher rates (12%) than girls of any other race or ethnicity and most boys; American Indian and Native-Alaskan girls (7%) are suspended at higher rates than White boys (6%) or girls (2%).

- **Disproportionate suspension rates, by race, sex, and disability status combined (see Figure B-4):** With the exception of Latino and Asian American students, more than one out of four boys of color with disabilities (served by IDEA)—and nearly one in five girls of color with disabilities—receives an out-of-school suspension. (p. 1)

The overrepresentation of students of color facing punitive discipline measures also feeds into the school-to-prison pipeline (Marsh, 2017), a pattern in which punitive, rather than supportive, disciplinary practices and policies in schools push students—especially those from marginalized communities—into the criminal justice system, potentially perpetuating a cycle of incarceration. What's more, Marsh goes on to write, "rather than making communities inside and outside school safer, there exists a growing consensus among educators, criminologists, and medical professionals that punitive discipline in fact increases the misbehaviors and violence that zero tolerance policies were intended to curb" (p. 3).

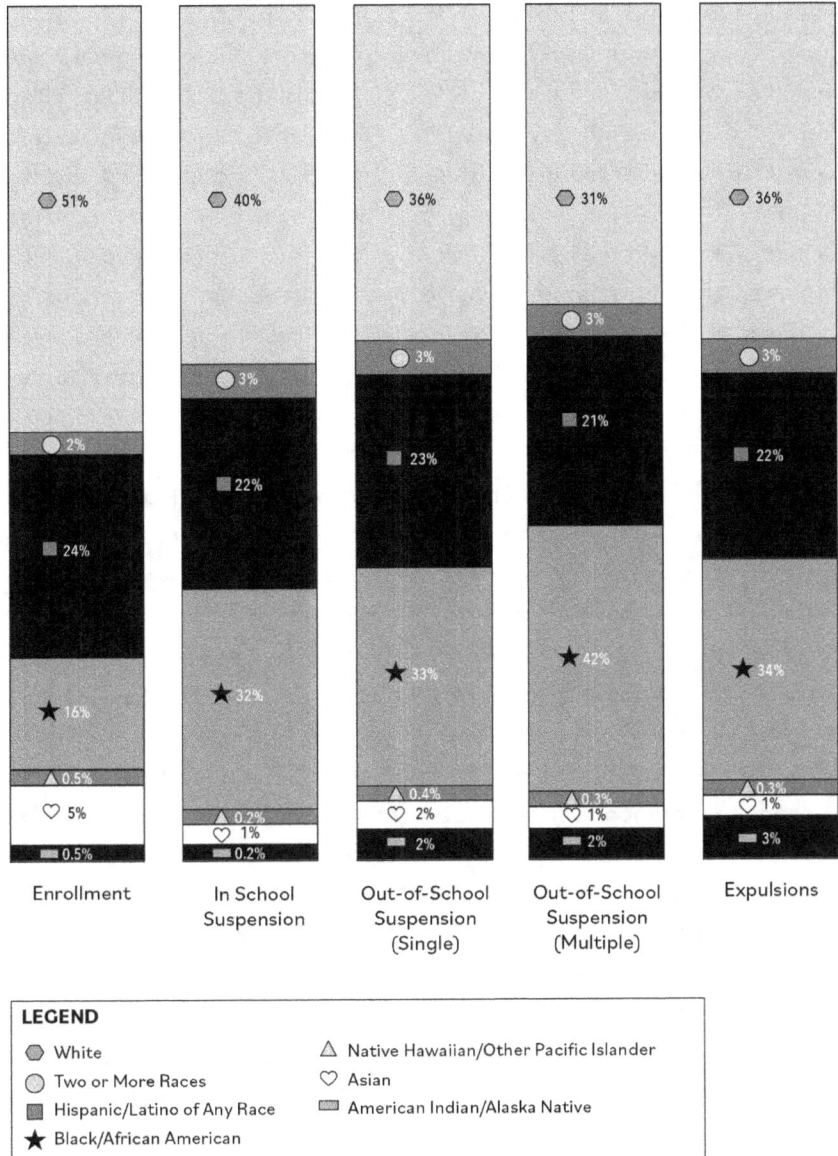

FIGURE B-4: Students receiving suspensions and expulsions, by race and ethnicity (source: U.S. Department of Education Office for Civil Rights, Civil Rights Data Collection, 2011–12)

As a result, educators, policymakers, and even the American Psychological Association began to move away from zero-tolerance, punitive measures to a focus on preventive strategies, alternatives to exclusionary measures, and culturally relevant training (American Psychological Association Zero Tolerance Task Force, 2008). Part of those disciplinary alternatives included restorative practices. Restorative practices in schools were first implemented in Australia in the 1990s (Blood & Thorsborne, 2005; Pratt, 1996) and eventually took hold in several other countries, including the United States. These approaches have been gaining traction as an alternative, more inclusive measure in educational settings.

Prior to their use in schools, restorative justice approaches were being utilized in pockets of the criminal justice system (*restorative justice* rather than *restorative practices* was and still is the more commonly used term in these settings). According to Armour (2012), restorative justice as a field in the Western world can be traced back to the 1970s, when alternatives to traditional court processes were increasing in popularity. This coincided with the victims' rights movement, which involved victims of crimes having a role in the criminal justice process. Armour describes the "Kitchener experiment," named after a 1974 case in Kitchener, Ontario, in which two teenagers were required to meet with and repay 22 victims whose property they had vandalized, as "the beginning point of today's restorative justice movement." Taking their cue from the Kitchener experiment, various experimental programs were developed in pockets of criminal justice systems in North America and Europe.

A turning point in restorative justice's impact at a system-wide level occurred in 1994 when the American Bar Association endorsed victim–offender mediation. From there, several organizations—including the National Organization for Victim Assistance, the United Nations, the Council of Europe, and the European Union—expressed a commitment to promoting restorative justice. In 2008, the American Bar Association began offering grants for restorative justice initiatives in criminal law settings, which further bolstered the popularity of restorative justice at an institutional level (Armour, 2012).

15

A Restorative Journey

SEAN GUTHRIE

Let's take a moment to hear from one of our former colleagues, Sean Guthrie, who was a math teacher and teacher leader at the Putnam Avenue Upper School. Sean brought his experience running a Sankofa Rites of Passage program at a Boston Public School to Putnam Ave., and he was one of the first teachers to volunteer when we began piloting restorative practices there. Sean's own experience of connecting with his Indigenous roots in Fiji played an integral role not only in his own identity development but also in his work and relationships with his students.

After being in education for more than 12 years, I took a trip that would help me to understand where my communal teaching style came from. My mother grew up in the islands of Fiji. When I was growing up, she would tell me about her island, but her stories were like fairy tales of a distant place that I would never see. Then one day, out of the blue, my mother told me she wanted to take me and my oldest daughter to Fiji to see where she had grown up. I was excited to go and didn't know what to expect. My mom hadn't been back to Fiji since she'd left over 40 years ago. I began to wonder if her family would welcome me as one of them. Would they accept a half Black, half Fijian?

My questions were answered as soon as I reached Fiji. When we finally arrived after an 18-hour plane ride, we were escorted to the president of Fiji's home. As we pulled up to the beautiful property filled with exotic trees and perfectly manicured lawns, I was taken aback by all the people waiting to greet us at the top of the hill. The hill was crowned with a white Victorian mansion that somehow fit this tropical paradise. As we got out of the black SUVs, we were greeted with leis and hugs from a line of relatives and family friends whom I had never known of. The welcoming feeling of belonging was something I hadn't felt before. It was more than being welcomed by family; it was a feeling of being welcomed by a nation.

I would have been overjoyed had this concluded my welcoming, but it did not. After greetings and getting to talk to President Jioji Konrote and his wife, my mother's cousin Sarote, I was led to an outdoor area and taken into a *mamasa*, a Rotuman ceremony traditionally held for fishermen who had been out at sea for many days. The mamasa was a way of welcoming the fishermen back home and honoring them for the work they had done to feed the community. Over the years, this ceremony has been used to honor anyone who has been away for a long time, and in this case, it was being held to welcome my mother back home. As I entered the circle where everyone—including the president—was seated, I was given a *sulu*, a wrap worn around the waist like a skirt, to put on. The sulu had a beautiful floral design. I was then asked to take off my shirt and sit next to my mother and daughter in this circle. The president, his wife, and many other dignitaries were sitting on mats that had been spread on the floor under the tent. It felt strange yet somehow familiar sitting in that circle with my shirt off, listening to the president and others welcoming my mother, daughter, and me into the community and back home. Even though I had never been to Fiji, I felt like I was home by the end of that ceremony.

I was introduced to restorative practices going into my fourth year of teaching when I was at South Boston High School. I was a math teacher and football coach. This was a natural fit for me, as I was an accounting major and had risen to the heights of the NFL in my athletic journey. Because of these two roles, young men tended to gravitate toward me, and I had developed a reputation for being able to reach the most difficult male students. These qualities led to my principal introducing me to the Sankofa Rites of Passage program. This program was different from anything I had been a part of yet also strangely familiar. It wasn't until years later that I realized the connections between my Polynesian roots, the Sankofa Rites of Passage, and restorative practices.

The premise around Sankofa draws upon African traditions to guide young men through their rites of passage into manhood. The boys selected for this program were students who were having behavioral challenges in school. All of the boys that were a part of Sankofa had been suspended multiple times during the school year. My goal for them was to help build up their self-esteem culturally and as individuals. As I got to know the young men better, I soon realized that trauma was a common theme among them. One of the by-products of their experiences with trauma was not having healthy strategies when they found themselves in situations involving conflict. Most situations involved the feeling of not being respected.

Restorative practices are about healing, about helping individuals and communities return to the healthy place they once were. The young men that I worked with were at one point emotionally healthy but experienced trauma that taught them to react to conflict in physically and verbally combative ways. This trauma ranged from parental abuse to witnessing violence in their neighborhoods. To begin the restorative process, we began each class together in circles, invoking the feeling of appreciation through libations. During libations, we would give honor unto our ancestors. We would give thanks to parents, grandparents, uncles, aunts, older cousins, great-grandparents, historical figures, unknown ancestors, and anyone else who played a significant role in the young men's life. This daily ritual helped teach us how to come together in a circle and open up our hearts to give thanks for those who came before us. Libations, the beginning of our collective healing, shifted our focus from what we didn't have and the people who had wronged us to the people and things we were appreciative of.

I would learn through this process that one of the keys to restorative practices is a shift in mentality and orientation. I would learn that restorative practices are not effective on a systemic level when this critical shift does not happen. I would also learn how important building up cultural and individual self-esteem is to restorative practices. When conflict would arise between the young men, it was very difficult to sit them down and have them talk through the issue at hand, and to get them to an authentic space where the situation was really resolved. These conversations would serve as a Band-Aid to get us past the moment, but when the situation arose again, the wound would reopen and we would be right back where we started.

This is why our identity work was so important: to get us to a space where we could come together as a community and be able to speak from the heart about situations of conflict so that all parties involved were able to walk away from the conversation feeling whole. We took time each week to set goals and identify different qualities about ourselves that we were proud of. I paid close attention to each young man to help him identify his talents. Many of the young men I worked with had been given so much negative feedback that it was hard for them to see, much less cultivate, their positive attributes, resulting in them misusing those qualities and finding themselves in trouble. Reminding these young men about their brilliance helped me to create a space of hope and healing.

16

Pause and Reflect On Part B

SUMMARY

Restorative practices are a framework and range of approaches that aim to develop community and manage conflict and tensions by repairing harm and restoring relationships. Restorative practices are *not* simply a checklist of strategies but instead involve an entire way of being and believing. As their roots in and influences from Indigenous cultures around the world illustrate, these practices must be firmly grounded in belief systems that center community and healing. Practically speaking, schools that wish to incorporate a restorative practices framework and approach should focus on developing proactive, tier 1 efforts that foster and strengthen relationships within the classroom and the larger school community. The more solid the tier 1 practices are, the less effort schools will have to expend on reactive tier 2 and 3 interventions. At their core, restorative practices should lift up student voices and prioritize issues of justice and equity.

REFLECTION QUESTIONS

1. How can you honor the Indigenous roots of restorative practices in your own learning and implementation journey? What might this look like on a personal or individual level and at the larger, school-wide level?

2. How can restorative practices help your school culture and community become more racially and socially just?

3. Why is it important to understand that restorative practices are a system of beliefs and a way of being rather than just a checklist of strategies? How can this ground you in your implementation journey?

4. Think about a setting where it might be appropriate to hold a tier 1 community-building circle. Use the Circle Planning Template in Table B-1 to guide you in your preparation.

PART C

The Power of Student Voice

To truly listen is to risk being changed forever.
—James Sákéj Youngblood Henderson,
Indigenous rights lawyer and advocate

17

Stories of Belonging . . . or Not

THE BARN

MIRKO CHARDIN

My wife, Hayley, and I love to visit a small brewery that we affectionately call "the Barn," although that's not the business's real name. The Barn is located about four towns over from where we live. We love the ambiance, food, staff, and service so much that we are willing to drive past several other options to get there, including a handful of other breweries that, to be honest, all have much better quality beer.

When we walk in, we are always greeted by name—"Hey, Mirko and Hayley, welcome back!"—and with a smile. How could you not fall in love with a place that always treats you like you're expected to arrive, like you're a part of the culture? Even though we visit the Barn more than our own dining room, they embrace variability and provide us with endless options. After being greeted and exchanging pleasantries, we are asked, "Outside or inside?" "At the bar or near the fireplace?" "Glass of water?"

Once Hayley and I are seated, the server always asks if we want our "usual" (a vodka raspberry lemonade sparkler and a Manhattan), a recommendation, or something new on the cocktail list that may have caught our eye. She asks us about work and our dog, Sebi, and laughs at all our jokes (I mean, we *are* funny!). And the food, don't even get me started. The stuffed pretzels are incredible.

The Barn is a place I want to be, a place that embraces who we are and treats us with respect and dignity. If you were to come visit us, that's where we would take you for a good time. For a moment, imagine sitting at the Barn with an icy cold glass, a warm fire, and five-star service. Now, we are going to ask you to imagine two very different experiences from Pam and Edgar.

CAN I TAKE YOUR ORDER?

PAM CHU-SHERIFF

Ask anyone who knows me, and they'll tell you that I love to eat. Anything fried, anything doused in chocolate, or any meat of the land, air, or sea variety, and I'm all in. Do I sometimes keep beef jerky on hand in my bag? Yes. Am I willing to travel over an hour to try out the latest iteration of brown sugar bubble tea? Of course. Is mac and cheese even better on top of a burger? Absolutely—are you kidding me?!

One thing I don't love, though, is waiting in line. And not for the reason you might think. I can be pretty patient when it comes to waiting for food, especially good food. But I do not have patience for racist, sexist shenanigans. As a five-foot-two-and-a-half Asian woman, I have become all too accustomed to standing dutifully in line only to have a server or cashier call on the person behind me or to the side of me even though it is clearly, objectively, my turn. When servers call out, "Next!" or "Can I take your order?" and look straight past me even though I'm standing right in front of them, there are not usually signs of malicious intent. I think most of these folks don't even realize that they instinctively wanted to help the tall male or the blonde woman first. It's just that *I am invisible to them*.

Many of us have heard of the body's fight, flight, or freeze response when we're faced with threatening situations. Now, I can show patience and grace when people make mistakes, but if someone is going to treat me like I don't exist because I'm Asian, because I'm a woman, or because I'm an Asian woman, then my knee-jerk reaction is to fight. As a former teacher and administrator who never has enough hands to carry everything, I've always used tote bags instead of purses in large part because tote bags can hold so many things. But I've also learned that tote bags are quite handy to use as a shield between me and the umpteenth customer who tries to plow their way over me or somehow insists on standing so far into my personal bubble that I can feel their breath in my ear. I've found that a sudden turn of the body with a giant tote slung over my shoulder just so is the perfect way to literally push back against someone who is in my space and send the message *Hey, I exist, so back off.* Other times, I am all too ready to tersely announce, "Actually, I'm next in line," with an eye roll so deep that I'm surprised my vision isn't permanently damaged at this point.

However, being constantly in fight mode is a sure pathway to fatigue. When I walk into a store knowing that nine times out of ten I will be ignored and then watch a customer before or after me who doesn't look like me being greeted with a friendly hello or a warm, "Can I help you with anything?" I'm already extremely on edge. I often brace myself for something to happen and try to have a comeback at the ready in case it does. The racism of invisibility leaves one fighting to be seen, and fighting is exhausting. So, when I'm too tired to act out, I'll usually check out instead. When we order food, I often ask my husband, a tall South Asian male, to pick it up for me (although he's often mistaken for a food delivery driver, so pick your poison) or to do the speaking when I don't have the energy. Or, we'll just cease frequenting those businesses altogether.

As educators, we are, in a sense, in the service industry in that we should see ourselves as being of service to our students. It is crucial that we treat them with the dignity and respect they so rightfully deserve. As a grown woman in my forties, I am inclined to act out or check out if I am treated poorly, regardless of intentions. How much more will our young people act out, check out, or worse if their learning environments are not designed to see them, hear their voices, or even greet them with a kind hello? And authentically, why would they trust the individuals who work in those spaces? And why would they be expected to, if as adults we would not be willing to subject ourselves to this treatment?

NO ONE INTERRUPTED MY DAYDREAM

EDGAR VASQUEZ

As a Latino man, I am conscious of the bias that some extend toward people who look like me, especially when it comes to making large purchases like a nice car. I parked my car on a side street to make sure that my older model vehicle would not be visible from the dealership windows. And with that, the anxiety of shopping for a new car began. Having gone through the experience before, I knew that the dealer would try to:

- get me to buy a car that is not in my budget,
- sell me something that is not what I am looking for, or
- get me to buy something that makes sense for them and that is in the best interest of their business.

All of these thoughts raced through my mind before I had even left my vehicle. When I finally felt composed enough to get out of the car, I walked slowly toward the dealership and began scanning the lot. I'd conducted research and traveled to this specific dealership because they had the car I wanted to purchase, an Audi Q5 3.0L.

As I neared the doors of the showroom, I noticed a single customer who was seated at a desk and engaged in conversation with a salesman. The rest of the showroom was empty. This gave me hope that I was going to be showered with undivided attention, that they'd listen to my wants and needs and fully understand what I was shopping for. Spoiler alert: This is not what happened.

I continued into the showroom and immediately began admiring the new cars. I daydreamed of cruising in the top-of-the-line model they had in the middle of the showroom floor: a luxury package Audi S8, with a sleek black exterior and black leather interior, large aluminum polished wheels, a high-definition 15-speaker stereo system, and a panoramic sunroof. I consider myself a car enthusiast, so I know about cars—their specs, packages, options, drivetrains, and performance. So I knew what this car could do.

I figured I'd sit in the car until someone greeted me or asked if I needed help. As I sat in the driver's seat, I became enamored by it all: the feel, the design, the comfort, the delicate upholstery, the high-end speaker system, and many other aspects of the car. I was like a kid in a toy store and expected someone to come over and say something like, "Pretty, awesome, huh?" or "You want to take it for a ride?" After a moment or so, I realized that no one was paying attention to me. No one interrupted my daydream. Since the dealership was virtually empty, I thought this was odd. I began to wonder if I was going to be approached by anyone who worked there.

Because no one connected with me, I started second-guessing everything. Was it something I did? Was I not dressed like someone they thought actually intended to purchase anything? I had just gotten off work, gone to the gym, and returned home to shower and put on comfy non-work clothes: sneakers, jeans, t-shirt, and a Boston Red Sox baseball cap.

The other customer was gone. Why did everyone treat me like I was invisible? Forty minutes later, after I had sat in three different cars in the showroom, I realized no one was going to attend to me or even acknowledge my visit.

Another customer, a White man also wearing casual clothes, walked in. Immediately, he was warmly greeted by not one employee, but two.

On my way out the door, a salesperson asked if I needed help. I was frustrated and shared that I had waited alone in the showroom for 40 minutes. He apologized and assured me that he'd assist in getting me the deal I was looking for. I quickly learned that the Audi I wanted was not even on their lot. He had no explanation for this and tried very hard to sell me two other vehicles that I had absolutely no interest in.

—

Are our schools and classrooms intentionally communicating to students that we see them, hear them, and value what they have to say? Or is it more often a circumstance like Edgar's visit to the dealership, where our learners come with a positive intent and excitement that is unintentionally but frequently met with a lack of acknowledgment, making them feel invisible?

Where would you rather be? At the Barn with Mirko, waiting in line for food with Pam, or looking for a car with Edgar? The answer is obvious. Just like our learners, we all want to be in spaces in which we are acknowledged and treated with respect and dignity, and it should be the same in schools as well.

18

Considering the Recipients of Our Service

How do businesses and organizations adapt to provide such personalized, targeted customer service? They consider the recipients of service as educators should consider students. They ask for feedback and they listen. As a consumer, we have so many options and choices to provide feedback to the businesses we patronize. We can complete surveys, post online reviews, and ask to talk to managers. In the business world, customer feedback is critical for customer satisfaction. In fact, research suggests that one of the most important drivers of satisfaction is having direct conversations with customers to determine their wants and how things are going (Schwager & Meyer, 2007). And great companies listen and change.

In our society and world, the old adage of "the customer is always right" rings true, so much so that many successful companies have utilized this motto as the cornerstone of their business model and philosophy. In fact, this has reaped so much success that customers now expect it as a universal norm. Why then does it not ring true in schools?

As educators, we have customers and clients—our students and families—and they should be afforded the same respect, dignity, and customer service that they'd receive in the most responsive and inclusive places of business. Greeting students and families as they arrive at school in kind and welcoming ways, showing them that we are aware of their preferences, providing them with choices and options, and being open to feedback will make the experience of coming to school feel more like the Barn than the car dealership.

Our schools and districts need to focus on the customer experience and must seek to serve all students, their families, and their communities. To make these shifts, school leaders and educators need to genuinely listen to their customers and clients while being incredibly responsive to their feedback. In a universally designed system, it is critical that we create spaces for students to feel safe enough to share their voice, and educators have to be ready and willing to change in response to that. Again, we speak from experience here and not solely through a theoretical lens. At Mirko and Pam's school, there were multiple opportunities for individuals to provide feedback in ways that worked for them as well as a commitment from leadership to address and respond to all feedback, including critical feedback, publicly. As leaders, if anyone was going to trust us, we had to first model vulnerability and accountability through transparency so that our folks could take a chance in trusting us—not because of what we said, but because our actions communicated that we were trustworthy and that our intent was to listen and do our best to take action in response to what we heard.

19

Cogenerative Dialogues (Cogens)

Educators can gather student voice and critical feedback on practice by instituting what Dr. Christopher Emdin has coined "cogenerative (cogen) dialogues." According to Dr. Emdin:

> *Cogens are simple conversations between the teacher and their students with a goal of co-creating/generating plans of action for improving the classroom. . . . They allow teachers to more effectively deliver complex subject matter to students to bridge their cultural divides before addressing content. . . . [In] instances where the youth and the teacher are from different cultural backgrounds . . . effectively introducing and implementing the cogen . . . has proven to be effective in motivating students to engage in dialogues with teachers in ways that allow them to share with their teachers their suggestions for improving the classroom. (2016, p. 66)*

Cogens are facilitated conversations about the inner workings of spaces, like classrooms, where people cohabit. We present this strategy to you as a form of restorative practice, considering the fact that it provides agency and voice to your learners. Along the continuum of restorative practices (see Figure B-1), cogens would fall under the category of formal structures. Cogens welcome self-expression and value the voice of the student as well as students' critiques of the classroom. In short, teachers authentically listen to students and then make instructional moves to incorporate their feedback.

If we truly value our students and see them as our customers and clients, we have to be willing to institute restorative structures such as cogen groups as a means of gathering feedback from them to inform our practice and classroom decision-making. By communicating to students that not only will we hear their voices about what they need, but we will also make efforts to respond to and incorporate their feedback into our practice, we are showing that their voice has value and matters.

It may be difficult to visualize a cogen dialogue and understand its power. In this next section, we offer an example of a student, whom we'll call Arnold, who was empowered through cogen dialogues. As you read about Arnold's journey, consider how his experience shifted from one akin to being ignored in line or at a car dealership to one that was more like being at the Barn.

"Y'ALL DON'T LISTEN": COGENS AT WORK

MIRKO CHARDIN

Arnold came to the Putnam Avenue Upper School in Grade 6. He was small for his age but made up for it with clothes three sizes too big, borrowed from his older brother. He puffed out his chest when he stepped off the bus every morning. He often greeted the administrative team with a nod of his head or a fist bump. When Arnold was in eighth grade, he was sent to the office, which triggered restorative practice protocols. As soon as students are regulated, they are encouraged to write or draw about what happened, their intentions, the outcome, and their thoughts about what should happen next. Once students have had an opportunity to reflect, the student and a staff member have a conversation.

When Arnold walked in, I did a double take. I was shocked, as this young man had never been sent to the office before. I knew him well and had a positive relationship with him. I knew he was a huge New England Patriots fan, loved music by Lil Baby, and was the youngest of three siblings. I was often concerned that he was not applying himself or working as hard as he could, but no matter how many times I had convinced myself that I would follow up with him to try to push him, there was always something else that pulled my attention in another direction. There were emails to answer, meetings to attend, and educator observations to log. Clearly, all of this was important work, but it did not put Arnold first.

Once he was in my office, I let him know that I was disappointed but that I also held myself responsible because I cared about him and was aware for a while now that he was not working as hard as I knew he could. I apologized that I let my schedule get too busy to let him know this. As a school leader, I am responsible for the culture and the climate of the school, as well as the experiences of all the customers. I wanted him to know that we both could grow from the experience.

I also stressed that although he would receive a consequence for his actions, the incident was not a reflection of how I saw him and I would not hold it against him. In fact, I wanted him to know that I would try to have his back if he needed or wanted that. I stressed it would be a team effort to support, reflect, grow, and apply ourselves differently.

From my perspective, I was nailing it. Everything I did was by the book. I went on to remind him that we are a restorative practices school, shared some authentic micro-affirmations about his potential, and committed to having his back. I felt good about myself and thought I probably surprised him by not being upset and expressing faith in him.

I smiled triumphantly, thinking to myself, *I know this kid; he's going to apologize, and then I'll work on getting him a tutor to help get his grades up.* I had a plan, great intentions, and I was sure that the impact of my words was spot on.

I then asked Arnold what he thought.

"You lying," he said. "The adults here be cool, say cool things, but it's still wack, 'cause y'all don't listen."

My emotional energy shifted. The stern disciplinarian in me awoke. Arnold was crossing the line.

"No one asked me nothing. Y'all don't know what happened or why. Not even you, Mr., and you're supposed to be better than all of 'em. We supposed to be able to trust and count on you. . . ."

As much as I wanted to dish out a consequence, I took a deep breath and said, "Arnold, tell me what happened."

Arnold told me he'd been up late the night before. His mom was sick, and it was his responsibility to help out and watch his little brother when she couldn't. He told me the class he was in was super boring, and he had his head down as he was reading. The teacher thought he was sleeping and grabbed his backpack off the floor and slammed it down on his desk. When that happened, one of the buckles on his bag hit him in the face. He knew the teacher didn't do it on purpose, but it hurt when he got hit, and he reacted. He jumped and yelled, "F–ing b—." The teacher kicked him out.

My stomach turned. I was sitting face-to-face with a customer, my student, whom I had known for several years, as he shared about not feeling seen or heard. It clicked for me that this had to be connected to him not applying himself. I also knew that if the teacher who sent him to the office had heard his story, the teacher would have responded differently. So, before asking Arnold what he thought should happen next, I made a recommendation.

"Arnold, I'm sorry about the situation that took place. I'm sorry that the bag made contact with you. You need to see the nurse or anything? Because after that, I would like us both to have a conversation with the teacher."

The teacher took it even worse than I did. He felt so bad about what happened and was very open to engaging in a restorative conference with Arnold as well as starting a cogen group for his class. Once the three of us were back in my office, I invited Arnold to speak first and to share what he remembered about the incident. After hearing his words, the teacher apologized, and Arnold did too. The teacher then shared with Arnold that he was looking for a small group of student volunteers to give him feedback and suggestions on how class was going and he wanted to know if Arnold would be a part of it. Arnold accepted, but only if the teacher would listen to his suggestions on how to make the class less boring. That was the first cogen group that Arnold participated in, and it changed who he was as a student. Moving forward, he was more engaged and more present, and his grades went from a 70 average to the high 90s.

Even with all of my training and belief in the power of student voice, I had not put a structure in place to really hear Arnold's voice. I truly believe that the voices of our learners should drive the school experience, but I will admit, in that moment, I did not act that way. Having restorative structures and policies does not ensure that students will be heard if we don't commit and recommit to them every day. Participating in a cogen group after this amplified for Arnold that he had a voice, that it mattered, and that by using it, he could improve things for himself and for his classmates. We showed him that the customer was right.

20

Steps to Implementing Cogen Groups

As an educator, you might struggle to determine how to facilitate cogen dialogues in ways that can honor students, help them feel heard, and improve your practice. As experienced practitioners in restorative practices, we offer the following tips for you to begin your journey. Teachers can institute cogen groups by doing the following based on the work of Dr. Christopher Emdin (2016):

- Identifying volunteers based on differences in social, ethnic, or academic groups. The group should consist of both high-achieving and low-achieving students as well as both highly engaged and disengaged students.

- Accurately reflecting the diversity of the classroom. The differences revealed in the cogen are what leads to rich dialogue, which in turn leads to more opportunities for educators to understand the different realities of students in the classroom. Cogens should never be homogeneous.

- Inviting students to participate. Students should not feel pressured to take part and should be permitted to opt out.

- Introducing cogens in a way that does not make students see them as an additional classroom responsibility or assignment. Cogens should be framed as a privilege, not a punishment. Tailor invitations to each individual student; allow students' input in terms of when the dialogues will take place.
- Planning the initial dialogue over a meal or snack.
- Establishing rules and norms during the first dialogue. For example:
  - No voice is privileged over another.
  - One person speaks at a time.
- Ensuring that the cogen results in a plan of action to improve the classroom.
- Starting with a small issue that has an obvious easy answer so that the group can solve it together in order to ensure a positive experience for them.
- Involving new voices. The initial group should meet three or four times max, and then you should ask students to invite one or two new students to join and allow an existing member to opt out. This keeps the group small and provides opportunities to include new voices.

Table C-1 summarizes these steps for setting up and implementing a cogen group.

TABLE C-1: Steps to Implementing Cogen Groups (Adapted From Emdin, 2016).

STEP	DESCRIPTION
1: Identify participants.	Select participants with diverse backgrounds, including social, ethnic, and academic differences. Include high-achieving, low-achieving, highly engaged, and disengaged students.
2: Create diversity.	Build cogen groups that accurately mirror the diversity within your classroom. This diversity fuels richer conversations and insights into different student realities.

STEP	DESCRIPTION
3: Invite participation.	Extend voluntary invitations to students. Make it clear that participation is optional and there is no pressure to join.
4: Introduce cogen groups.	Present cogen groups as a privilege, not an additional assignment. Tailor invitations to individual students and involve them in deciding dialogue timings.
5: Plan the initial dialogue.	Schedule the first dialogue over a meal or snack. This casual setting encourages a relaxed and open atmosphere for discussions.
6: Establish rules and norms.	Set ground rules or norms at the start of the first dialogue. Examples include prioritizing every voice equally, speaking one at a time, and ensuring actionable outcomes.
7: Start with a small issue.	Begin with a straightforward issue that has a clear solution. Early success builds confidence and sets a positive tone for future dialogues.
8: Involve new voices.	After initial meetings, have existing members invite one or two new students while a current member opts out. This rotation keeps the group fresh and diverse, inviting new perspectives.

Implementing cogen groups fosters open communication, trust-building, and a sense of value among students. Remember that ongoing commitment and adaptability are key to maintaining the effectiveness of cogen groups in accommodating changing classroom dynamics. As you embark on this journey, you enhance your teaching practice and create a more inclusive and enriching educational experience for all. Remember, if students are at the center, then we have mechanisms in place that help us listen to what they have to say.

21

Honoring Student Voices

Education research has long neglected to include the voices of the very students that the research is purportedly and ultimately designed to serve. Brasof and Levitan (2022) describe how this dearth of young people's involvement extends not only to the field of education research but also to the academic, policy, and practitioner worlds. However, the burgeoning field of student voice research has shown that centering students' experiences and hearing from students themselves provides invaluable insight into a host of educational issues, from behavior challenges and student engagement to social justice issues and solutions.

While student voice research tends to focus on aspects of engagement and civic involvement, Dr. Joseph Kahne and his team of researchers at the University of California, Riverside, and Northwestern University found academic benefits to incorporating student voice as well. In a study published in the *American Journal of Education*, Kahne's team analyzed survey responses and academic data from 12,000 ninth-grade students enrolled in the Chicago Public Schools during the 2018–19 school year. Their study was the first of its size to utilize panel data to examine the relationships between responsiveness to student voice and academic performance (Kahne et al., 2022). They found that in schools where students felt that their voices were being heard—if the school leaders and teachers were "responsive"—the students had better grades and attendance and reduced rates of chronic absenteeism. As you delve deeper into the journey through this text, you will see these findings reinforced through our own lived experiences as well as those of several of our colleagues who have reaped the benefits of healing their school communities by implementing restorative practices to center student voice.

Similarly, restorative practices and circles wouldn't have a leg to stand on if not for their emphasis on hearing from a multitude of voices, in particular those that have traditionally been silenced or marginalized. As we have highlighted, restorative practices not only encourage dialogue and discussion but also involve students in the decision-making process. Enlisting students in these processes can take a multitude of forms, such as having them create their own circle guidelines, participate in cogens, tell their stories of self, lead circles of their peers, or brainstorm next steps after an incident in which a member of the community has been harmed. The list goes on!

In addition, we can't forget how important student voice and feedback are in terms of improving our own practice. Educators across the nation, from districts in Washington State to those in Massachusetts, are grappling with this work but also experiencing success. As educational consultants, Mirko and Pam have the luxury of working with teachers, support staff, and administrators as they engage in this type of work.

For instance, Mirko was recently in the Pacific Northwest working with a small district located 40 minutes or so outside of Seattle. A group of sixth graders from across the district was brought together to share their thoughts with district leadership about the district's fifth-to-sixth-grade transition activities and to help brainstorm an approach that, from their perspectives, would've better met their needs. It was powerful to see the young people go from being bashful about expressing their thoughts to, over the course of the session, sharing very pointed feedback and ideas about how things could and should improve. The key factor is whether the adults, as part of their professional learning culture, are willing to normalize wrestling with questions such as: *Can we solicit mastery-oriented feedback from our students? Can we model vulnerability and self-reflection by setting up cogens with our students?*

We could not write a text about tools and mechanisms to center students' voices without actually hearing from those voices. Next, we will share what some current and former students have to say about this work, their experiences with it, and what it has meant to them. These are the voices of two of Edgar's students from Boston Arts Academy who have been empowered by going to a school with a universally designed culture of restorative practices.

EMILY, BOSTON ARTS ACADEMY

(This transcribed interview has been edited for clarity and length.)

Please introduce yourself! Tell us about your background and interests.

Hi, my name is Emily. I'm a tenth-grade graphic designer at Boston Arts Academy. I'm Dominican and Puerto Rican, and some of my interests are painting, getting extra education, and learning how to do bouquets and stuff. I have a lot of interest in that.

What do you think are the benefits of circles and restorative practices?

I would say the benefits of circles and restorative practices are that everybody can speak and everybody can have their voice heard. Everybody can talk about the situation, and the situation gets talked about.

Can you share an example of a time when you were part of a powerful circle?

An example of a time where I was a part of a powerful circle was like a month ago. There was a certain situation that happened in my classroom, and we had a circle. I feel like it was so powerful because everybody had a chance to talk about how they felt, and everybody was listening to each other. I felt the energy of the circle, and it felt really amazing.

How do circles allow students' voices to be heard?

If there wasn't an opportunity for circles, certain situations would just get played out for too long, and the tension that is built up from that situation could cause so much worse than what had already happened. Circles allow things to be—what's that saying?—like, nip it in the bud, for it to cut off and [be] done with. Circles allow students' voices to be heard by them being able to express how they feel, how they want to be heard. They are given an opportunity to speak so nobody speaks over them, and they really have the floor.

IDEAL, BOSTON ARTS ACADEMY

(This transcribed interview has been edited for clarity and length.)

Please introduce yourself! Tell us about your background and interests.

Hi, my name is Ideal. I'm currently an alumni from Boston Arts Academy. I'm Cape Verdean and Black. Some things that I do as a hobby and what interests me right now: I have my own business, and I do a lot of other entrepreneurial things, like cutting hair. I sew clothes. I do a lot of hands-on activities.

What do you think are the benefits of circles and restorative practices?

I remember in high school, I was a part of a team called the Emerging Leaders that Mr. Vasquez created to better the community inside of the school atmosphere. One thing that we did there a lot was we had collective group circles. It was like circles to restore that school atmosphere and what was going on around school. I definitely think that having restorative circles and talks like that do help a community.

Can you share an example of a time when you were part of a powerful circle?

For instance, I remember in high school there was a situation where lunch was about to be put inside of classrooms because the kids didn't know how to act during the actual lunch setting. One way that we fixed that is we continuously met every two weeks or something like that. And then we literally sat in a circle with the Emerging Leaders and came up with different steps that can help better the community and helped actually start doing these types of circles in classes. So this incident wasn't just a one-time ordeal but actually ended with a discussion on how people felt and opened up a discussion on how people are feeling.

What do you think are the benefits of circles and restorative practices?

It just gives everyone a better understanding of the space and the atmosphere before students even step into the class or of what they will be learning for the day because then teachers could get to see where different students are coming from and how they are feeling for the day. And teachers can know, *Oh, maybe I shouldn't be so hard on this student that I'm usually hard on today because he communicated in the circle that his morning was rough,* and all these things.

How do circles allow students' voices to be heard?

So restorative circles really do work. They help build a community no matter what because everybody's voices are being heard and everyone is contributing to the circle. It definitely helps voice the opinion of every student on how they're feeling or what they're going through. Or you can even open up a lot of them with games to change the energy in the room. So I think it's very beneficial for students. Thank you!

22

Using Restorative Practices for Teaching and Learning

Research in social-emotional learning and neuroscience tells us that students need to feel a sense of safety in order to take in and process new information. Asking a question, volunteering an answer, expressing that they need help, or trying something new can be intimidating for some and downright scary for others. These fears may lead to that dreaded "amygdala hijack" if we as educators are not careful. We must view the classroom as a safe space for a community of learners instead of, say, simply a room located in our building. As we've learned, restorative practices and circles are an effective means of building that essential sense of community. Yet an often overlooked benefit of restorative practices and circles is that they can also help to create a safe space for students as they take on the emotional risks that might come with learning academic content.

We already know that circles are designed to center student voice. With practice, they can encourage fuller, more authentic participation. For students who tend to take up more airtime, circles encourage them to practice listening; on the other hand, for students who tend to be quieter, circle structure can encourage them to use their voices within a predictable protocol (Boyes-Watson & Pranis, 2015).

Boyes-Watson and Pranis write, "The value of Circle as a pedagogical tool is nearly limitless" (2015, p. 69). They suggest that circles can be used in the classroom to

- check for understanding,
- learn new vocabulary,
- share reflections,
- identify areas of strengths and weaknesses in a given subject,
- reflect on struggles, and
- develop tips and strategies.

It is important to note, however, that circles should not be used for assessment purposes, and students should not be rewarded or penalized based on participation (2015).

Table C-2 is a Content Circle Planning template that can be used as a pedagogical tool for anyone interested in exploring circles. You can adapt this template to whatever lesson plan templates you prefer or are required by your school to use.

TABLE C-2: Content Circle Planning Template

Grade/class:	Unit/topic:
Objectives:	Standard:
Materials:	Preparation:
Opening:	
Check-in:	
Guidelines/values:	
Discussion rounds:	
Check-out:	
Closing:	

Depending on the time available, you do not have to do a deep dive into all of the circle components, and you can always trim them down. For instance, it's more than okay to pass on reviewing the guidelines, especially if your class is quite familiar with them already (although it doesn't hurt to have them posted around the room or projected onto a slide!). Your opening could be something as simple as modifying your Do Now/Activator or having students journal their responses. The check-out could involve a one-word answer. For example: "On a scale of 1 to 10, how did you like today's circle?" or "Share one word that describes how you're feeling right now."

In your planning, don't forget about the UDL principles of engagement, representation, and action and expression, which can be found in Chapter 39. What opening can you design to pique student interest so that they are poised to engage in the circle? Ask yourself: Can I present the different components of the circle in different ways? Perhaps you can project a portion or all of the circle onto slides. As you consider how students can demonstrate what they know, perhaps you can provide them with individual whiteboards and dry-erase markers to use during the check-out or the closing. Remember, the variations are endless, so be creative and have fun!

If you're struggling to imagine how a lesson can be designed using this template, take a moment to review the work of our colleague, Chris Godfrey, a former math educator at the Putnam Avenue Upper School, who incorporates restorative practices into his academic instruction (see Table C-3).

To reinforce that the expertise that drives this text is based on actual lived practitioner experiences and not solely on theory, we've invited two former colleagues, who were both math teachers at the Putnam Avenue Upper School, to share. First, we'll hear from Kareem Cutler, a sixth-grade math teacher, who used Math Talks and content circles to elicit student voice in a structured way. Math Talks are structured discussions focused on math concepts, problems, or strategies that encourage students to explain their reasoning, share different approaches, and engage in collaborative problem-solving to deepen understanding and critical thinking. These opportunities for student voice in an academic context helped to pave the way for increased student engagement.

TABLE C-3: Circle Planning Sample From Chris Godfrey

Grade/class: 7th Grade Mathematics	Unit/topic: Pre-alegbra
Objectives: Students will be able to reflect on their most recent benchmark assessment by viewing data and participating in a circle in order to craft a personal improvement plan.	**Standard:** 7.E.E.B.4.a Solve word problems leading to equations of the form $px + q = r$ and $p(x + q) = r$, where p, q, and r are specific rational numbers. Solve equations of these forms fluently.
Materials: Talking piece: Plush Amibo Yoshi Doll	**Preparation:** • Arrange chairs in a circle • Post Circle Guidelines • Distribute test results and planning guide
Opening: Share a time where you laughed a lot.	
Check-in: Choose a color that BEST describes how your day has gone. Be prepared to explain your answer.	
Guidelines/values: • Respect the talking piece. • Remain in the circle. • Speak from the heart. • Keep It Moving/Say Just Enough	
Discussion rounds: What do you notice about the data? What do you wonder? After viewing your own personal data, what went well? What might need to change?	
Check-out: Something I can't do now, but would like to be able to do by the end of this school year is . . .	
Closing: "There is no failure. Only feedback." —Robert Allen	

Then we'll hear from Chris Godfrey, whose circle planning sample you just saw, about how being mindful of the ways his teachers turned his experience around when he was a student learner—specifically, by including and making space for his voice—inspired him to become a math teacher and to do the same for his learners.

23

Using Restorative Practices for Learner Agency: Math Talks

KAREEM CUTLER

Students are rarely asked to put away their paper and pencil in a math class. I continued my instructions, "Please bring your chairs from behind the desk to form a mini-audience-style seating at the front of the class." My students all moved swiftly but were unaware of what activity was to come. I heard an excited "We're playing a game" from one student, and a hopeless "No, Mr. Cutler does not play games that much" from another student. "Maybe we're in trouble again," said the regular class entertainer, followed by "Quiet, so he can explain" from the row in the back. I grabbed their attention, "Eyes up in 3, 2, 1." Immediately everyone went silent.

Math Talks were introduced to me as a conversation starter for students to have the chance to share their strategies for all to hear, to normalize making their thinking visible, and to assist them with becoming self-reflective. I was told that the activity would highlight and improve my students' math thinking process; enable them to engage in verbal communication around math skills; and be restorative or healing for them by allowing them to use their voices, self-evaluate, and reflect in a safe way. Initially, I felt this was another activity I would have to implement in my class that would take away from my ability to ensure students gained the curriculum knowledge. I was reluctant to even listen to the remaining parts of the professional learning session, as I could only envision how Math Talks would not work or be helpful for my students.

After my internal struggle with the information, I returned to my optimistic mindset. The upside was the chance to establish student discourse, which was one of my goals that teaching year. I believed in helping students connect with math in positive ways, even if their previous experiences with math weren't that positive. So, hopeful that this strategy could restore my learners' sense of self and self-esteem as students capable of doing math, no matter what their past circumstances were, I dug into how to modify these Math Talks to fit my style in the classroom. Shockingly enough, as the foundational piece of the routine became ingrained into my lessons, it molded me into a better educator. The transformation of my math class began once Math Talks became an established instrument within my craft.

Math Talks required me to present norms. Once everyone was attentive, I said, "Okay, here's the plan for today. We all will have a chance to talk, and I would like for each person to share their lovely ideas. Before we begin, let's set the norms for this activity." This practice wasn't new for my class; it was usually developed earlier in the year. Our Math Talk norms were similar to those for the class: one voice at a time, respect opinions, and honor think time. I encouraged and praised my students often and proactively to encourage their participation.

After norms came the rules and instructions: "Circle up, and an image or problem will show on the front board; we are not going to yell out the answer or say anything quickly." To ensure everyone was still listening, I asked, "What are we not going to do?" "Yell out or say anything!" a few replied. I asked again, and more voices responded. "Once you see the image, you will have one minute of think time, and if you feel you have an answer, you will put your fist to your chest, like this," I explained as I demonstrated the action. I had the students repeat the motion of fist to chest twice more. Math Talks required the foundational setup of guidelines and clarity for everyone participating.

Most of the structure-building pieces were familiar to my classroom; however, the next part stretched my comfort zone. I called on a student who had a fist to their chest. "Please share how many dots you see," I said, as we all stared at the front-board image of dots in a 5×5 grid with a 3×3 area missing. "Sixteen, I think," the student nervously shared. "Louder, please, with confidence," I encouraged. "Sixteen," the student said more firmly.

My old teaching style was to move forward once I got the correct response, which created an unrecognized shortfall for all students. Yes, it's clear the student who shared knew the answer, and it's possible that the others who had a fist to their chest may also have had the correct response. However, moving on right away neglected the opportunity for that student to explain their thinking and share their voice for others to see the image in a new way. Also, my old ways commonly shut out students from engaging in processing their answers by not providing them with agency. Instead, as we sat in a tier 1 circle, our discourse moved fluidly and flexibly, both building community and reinforcing that it was okay for them to talk about math without shame or fear of judgment if they made a mistake or said the wrong thing.

Math Talks are meant to have many voices contribute to the discussion, presenting their answers in different ways from their own unique perspectives. That became true within every aspect of my lessons.

I called on another student, "How many?" "Twelve!" Then, I continued, "How many?" "Sixteen," the third respondent said. As I now looked at different students with eye contact, numbers flowed out—"fourteen," "twelve," "ten," "sixteen"—and surprisingly, no one felt wrong as they shared with confidence and I wrote each response on the board.

Next I had students share their way of seeing the dots. This is the tricky part. As the facilitator, I must be strategic in how I select students to share their ideas and recognize their errors or other ways of seeing the results. I chose the student who said 14, and she began with confidence as she guided me through circling the area where she noticed a cluster of

10 dots. Preparing scaffolding questions is vital to getting the students to explain their thinking. Once she concluded, I asked, "Can anyone express the dimensions we see for the area I circled?" This question challenged all students to process something different but relevant to simplify their thinking.

After a student's response, I asked, "How can we describe the missing area on this image?" A student yelled out, "Mr. Cutler, it's nine." "Nine what?" I replied. "Nine dots would be there." I did not shut the student down for not following our norms because I recognized it was a voice I didn't hear much, so I was happy for him.

Another important engagement tactic was to pass one student's response to another eager student leaning out of their seat. I gestured toward the excited student. "Please explain how you think he saw it was nine." Open-ended questions are intentional and purposeful, and enhance students' ability to explain their thinking using math terminology. I prepared the questions I'd anticipated I would ask in the same manner that I prepared questions for holding circles with discussion rounds. By the end of the session, 11 out of 20 students shared their voices, which I felt was successful for the first attempt especially since students who did not frequently talk became the front-runners during the explaining part.

Throughout the school year, I held Math Talks biweekly, then weekly, and, soon enough, every other day. The students felt it was a break from the usual math learning environment. In reality, I don't think they noticed, but most of my questioning and scaffolding during lessons embedded the techniques I'd gained by using Math Talks and the restorative circle format, tweaked for my purposes. It was a part of the class culture as students exchanged strategies, ideas, and their thinking during paired work time or openly during a whole-class review. I noticed my voice began to decrease over the year, and students were leading the conversations around more challenging problems presented within the curriculum, not just as a Math Talk problem. We normalized that it was okay to share their thoughts and voices.

I am thankful for gaining the ability to facilitate math dialogue and believe it was the essential ingredient in my teaching that enabled me to meet my goal of increasing student voice. The practice was healing and restorative and reinforced that even students who used to dread coming to math class could reclaim their agency by sharing their unique voices and methods of approaching the work. The math experience for my students was not odd anymore, as their brainpower had been expanded through the restorative and healing power of Math Talks.

24

From Finding Voice as a Learner to Finding Voice as a Teacher

CHRIS GODFREY

I hated math.

My earliest math memory begins in the seventh grade. At age 12, I had finally learned to multiply. Multiplication was not as convoluted of a process as it had been made to seem. In all transparency, I honestly wish someone would have just told me it was simply repeated addition. Although I was late to the party, my feelings on the subject of math shifted radically over the next few years of school.

During my eighth-grade year, I performed well and brought home a number of academic awards; however, nothing on the math side of things stands out in my mind. The following year in high school was more of the same. The pre-algebra class I was in was indeed memorable but for non-academic reasons. The work wasn't particularly challenging and most of the time we would recite lines from the movie *Friday* while completing the worksheets given out each class.

The apex of that journey was in tenth grade when Mr. Smith helped me create a bridge in my mind between art and math. You could chill for the last few minutes of his class if you completed everything he assigned, but it had to be on point. My friend Steven and I had made it a habit to complete our work so we could draw at the end of class. One day after a lesson on equations, Mr. Smith challenged Steven and me to re-create a drawing of our choice on a graphing calculator. Bet! Within minutes we were experimenting and had begun to reproduce Sonic the Hedgehog and MegaMan on our TI-83 calculators. Mr. Smith helped us with the equation for circles because that knowledge was outside the scope of the lesson, but we needed it to really push ourselves for this activity. He may or may not have done this intentionally, but Mr. Smith helped me see that I could use a strength of mine (art) to reclaim my voice and aid me in one of my weakest skills (math). It was OVER! This was a game-changer. A fire had been ignited.

The next few math teachers I encountered didn't go to the lengths that Mr. Smith did, but that didn't matter anymore. My angst and ire for math was dead. Although I didn't yet love the subject, I no longer hated it. I now knew that if and when trouble showed up for me in math, I could attack it and make sense of it with art, the way I expressed my voice and thoughts. This skill set would serve me well moving forward.

As I recalled these memories for my seventh-grade math students, there was a mixture of responses from the crowd. I took the time to illustrate these recollections and keep them short yet sweet. Some of these responses I had anticipated and others I had not. Based on the conditions in the communities where I grew up, I can often tell when someone's body language shifts. Being able to read people that way was vital to survival. In some faces, I read wonder and admiration; in others, disappointment. Being vulnerable is not something I rush to do, but I have learned of its value in terms of inspiring others. Modeling vulnerability was the norm at Putnam Ave., especially by sharing stories of self as a form of restorative practice and inviting my students to do so as well.

One response I didn't see coming was the willingness of one of my struggling mathematicians to begin coming for extra help after school. In sharing my story with the class, I guess it resonated with Isabelle. As a result, she started showing up consistently for additional support. After-school was more relaxed and so we would work, crack jokes, and talk about our lives outside of the building. Then one day it happened. As Isabelle was working on a math concept, it finally clicked! I will never forget the genuine smile that spread over her face. I asked her if I could take a picture of her and her work, and she agreed.

The whole purpose of summarizing and presenting those memories in that fashion was to help my students unlock that power in themselves. My goal wasn't that math become their favorite subject, but that they would no longer allow negative past experiences with teachers or the content prevent them from having and utilizing the skill set. It was important for them to know that it was okay to see themselves, be themselves; that sharing and connecting with stories about what we believe are our strengths and weaknesses is healing in that it helps us reclaim our voice and exercise agency by owning that voice and experience.

Later in the school year, when I presented new concepts that Isabelle would struggle or get frustrated with, I would pull out the photo of that day. She would still be super pissed off, but the picture and memory were helpful as they would help cut down the duration of the disruption.

By the end of the year, Isabelle had joined the Young People's Project, an organization that empowers young people, particularly from underserved communities, by providing them with math literacy and leadership skills; it is considered an outgrowth of the Algebra Project, founded by civil rights leader Bob Moses. Isabelle later became one of the leading students in the Math Playbook, a school-wide program that focused on student-led efforts to aid and support math teachers in engaging students around the subject.

From that point on, I leaned into being my authentic self and using my own voice while encouraging my students to do the same so that we could always find ways to connect and make math class our own.

25

Pause and Reflect On Part C

SUMMARY

Ultimately, we are called to create a learning environment that works for all students, regardless of variability. Student voice is critical. Without it, we are at risk of making students feel invisible, and the consequences are much more severe than walking away without a new car or being passed over in line. They will walk away without learning and without realizing how brilliant, celebrated, and valuable they are. Arnold's transformation, catalyzed by a cogen dialogue, is a testament to the potential of these facilitated conversations. They amplify student voices, bridge divides, and shape inclusive learning environments. This structured approach enables students to be heard, fostering collaboration between educators and learners in a shared quest for improvement. In the next chapter, we will further explore the practice Chris Godfrey mentioned—story of self—as well as personal narrative and their transformative connection to social-emotional learning.

REFLECTION QUESTIONS

1. In what ways have you witnessed or experienced the effects of invisibility and discrimination in education?

2. What steps can you take to actively counter biases and promote equitable treatment in your educational setting?

3. How might cogens transform your classrooms into spaces of collaboration and shared decision-making?

4. Have you truly listened to your students' voices, and how can you ensure they feel valued and heard?

5. What strategies can you employ to create a sense of privilege and honor around engaging in cogens?

6. How might the implementation of cogens impact students' sense of belonging and agency in the learning process?

PART D

Social-Emotional Learning Through Personal Narratives

If it is not relational, it is not justice.
—Kim Workman,
Maori criminal justice advocate

26

Story Time

PAM CHU-SHERIFF

The clock was ticking. It was almost 8 o'clock on this particular Friday morning in August, and I still hadn't plated the yogurt parfaits. I quickly finished slicing some hard-boiled eggs in half, sprinkled some freshly ground pepper and rock salt on top, and then got started on the parfaits. I turned on the jazz playlist I had curated and was scrambling to make sure there were enough utensils and napkins when the first guest walked through the door, several minutes early.

"Oh, hi! Welcome to the new teacher institute!" I called out cheerfully. "Help yourself to breakfast. Mirko made his special candied bacon if you're interested."

Thus began the annual first meeting of the Putnam Avenue Upper School's new staff institute, which would run over the course of the year. During this first meeting, themed "Welcome to the Family," we would spend time getting to know each other, review some housekeeping items (having a bathroom key was usually the top priority on everyone's lists), and then craft the content for our future meetings together; this would include work around restorative practices, writing objectives, the state's teacher evaluation system, and any other areas in which participants felt they could use support.

After everyone had settled into their seats and was busy munching away, Mirko and I went through the usual Putnam Ave. 101 basics: ice breaker activity, building tour, overview of the school's vision and values. Check, check, and check. Finally, it was time to move to the main focus of our meeting, "Educator Story Time." We asked everyone to respond to this question: What was your journey to education? Mirko and I went first, each sharing our own paths that led us to the field. Mirko opened up about his difficult upbringing in Boston and an arrest as a teenager; after multiple expulsions, he finally found a supportive school community that started him on the transformative path to becoming a teacher and administrator. I shared with the group about my adolescent struggles with identity as one of only a handful of students of color and one of the few children of immigrants in my school. After learning about Asian American history in college and becoming involved in community activism, I too was inspired—first in the classroom, and then as a school leader—to advocate for students on the margins.

Then, it was time to hear from our staff. We let people know to share as they felt comfortable, and as we went around the room, some described emotional journeys, while others touched upon humorous ones. One new staff member, recounting the day his father left the family, shared his father's parting words: "You're the man of the house now." The staff member described how this experience had forced him to develop a sense of responsibility and leadership qualities from a young age. Another staff member described coming from a long line of educators in their family and feeling called to the world of education, while another candidly shared how they fell into teaching after a career in field hockey didn't pan out.

In this informal, early morning circle, our hour of communal sharing helped to bring this new group of individuals closer. It also served as a primer for our school's larger Story of Self work, in which both teachers and students would engage in crafting their personal narratives in a structured and celebratory way. For us, this process was about the restorative power of personal narratives both to encourage and wrestle with the development of the Collaborative for Academic, Social, and Emotional

Learning's (CASEL's) five Social-Emotional Learning competencies: self-awareness, self-management, social awareness, relationship skills, and responsible decision-making. We highly recommend this approach for digging deeper into identity development and explorations of value systems.

27

Harnessing the Power of Personal Narratives

Of course, the act of sharing stories isn't merely a contemporary phenomenon; it's a practice that has pulsed through the veins of cultures for generations. For example, in many West African cultures, the role of *griot*, or storyteller, embodied what we believe is the essence of the restorative practice. The griot cradled the collective memory of their people. In the oral traditions maintained by griots, history wasn't held in solitude; it was a collective of voices that chronicled both victories and losses. In the flickering firelight of village gatherings, the griot's stories were more than entertainment; they were threads that stitched generations together. The act of listening wasn't passive; it was an active celebration of heritage, identity, and resilience.

Storytelling, in its myriad forms, holds the power to heal, to restore, and to unite. Sharing stories, much like restorative practices, involves collective reflection, sharing, listening, and social-emotional learning. The story of self, as coined by Marshall Ganz (2009), recognizes the transformative power of personal narratives in promoting connection, agency, and healing and fosters social-emotional skills such as self-awareness, self-management, social awareness, relationship skills, and responsible decision-making.

The Story of Self framework, much like the griots' tradition, uses personal narratives to both chronicle history and serve as a vehicle of empowerment. Just as the griot held the pulse of the community, Ganz's approach, which we will explore further in this part of the book, encourages individuals to delve into their own narratives by describing moments of challenge, choice, and change. These personal stories, once shared, are no longer solitary anecdotes; they become threads that weave through the fabric of collective struggles, aspirations, and triumphs. Extending these practices to include not only staff but also students, caregivers, and community members can dynamically transform and aid in the healing of entire school communities.

GANZ'S PUBLIC NARRATIVE FRAMEWORK

It is important to note that the griot, the educators of Putnam Avenue Upper School, and the work of Marshall Ganz all converge within the realm of Social-Emotional Learning (SEL), an educational paradigm that acknowledges the essential role of emotional intelligence, self-awareness, and interpersonal skills in fostering holistic growth.

The griot tradition, rooted in the heart of communities, serves as a precursor to the foundational tenets of SEL. Just as the griot's tales embodied empathy and unity, SEL encompasses the very essence of these values. The personal narratives shared by educators become not just stories but stepping stones for self-discovery and reclaiming voice and humanity. In the embrace of SEL, individual stories create opportunities for introspection, enabling educators to better understand themselves and thus better navigate the intricate dynamics of their classrooms and collaborations.

Ganz's call for harnessing the power of personal narratives is not a mere echo; it's a resonance that amplifies SEL. The educators' stories become more than instruments of inspiration; they exemplify self-awareness, they model vulnerability, and they underscore the importance of empathy. Just as Ganz's approach prompts individuals to connect their stories to larger narratives of change, SEL nurtures skills that encourage compassionate interaction, effective communication, and conflict resolution—a modern manifestation of the griot's ability to bind communities through shared stories.

Stories are tools of transformation. The narrative of the African griot weaves together the educators' anecdotes, all guided by the principles of SEL. This dynamic interaction creates a mosaic where history and contemporary pedagogy meet. SEL, much like the griot's tradition, paves a path toward emotional resilience, communal cohesion, and a restored sense of self and community. As educators embrace SEL, they not only continue the legacy of the ancient griot but also propel their students into a world where storytelling isn't just a practice but a way of nurturing empathy, understanding, and growth. Next we will delve even deeper into this connection by examining the story of a young person who was so positively impacted by experiencing a culture of universally designed restorative practices that it has echoed throughout his work and life ever since.

28

"I Am Because We Are": An Example of Personal Narrative

As we reflect upon the power of personal narratives, we now bring you the story of Ayo Lewis, who currently serves as the Youth Coordinator for the organization Restorative Justice for Oakland Youth (RJOY). Founded in 2005 by civil rights attorney Fania Davis, RJOY is a nonprofit organization based in Oakland, California, that aims to disrupt cycles of violence and incarceration by promoting restorative justice practices and policies in schools, communities, and the juvenile justice system. With a focus on racial justice consciousness, RJOY has been a national thought leader in the restorative justice movement. Ayo begins his story by sharing with us the challenges he faced as a high school student, the choices he made in the face of those challenges, and how he became a restorative justice practitioner himself after having experienced the power of these practices during his time as a student.

(This transcribed interview has been edited for clarity and length.)

Tell us about yourself! How did you become involved in restorative justice work?

My name is Ayo Lewis. I'm the youth coordinator at RJOY. I kind of fell into restorative justice in high school. I went to a high school out here that's famous for having pathways that can lead you into a career. I was in engineering and honors English. A lot of the famous pathways, like engineering and the honors English, were mostly White. The other ones were usually Black. Most of my classes, not even the pathways class but the rigorous classes in general—like AP Chem, AP Calc—they were mostly White. So most of the time, I was the only Black kid in my classes.

Throughout high school, I was just angry. I didn't even know necessarily what I was upset about. I just felt alone. I still had the grades and everything, but I was coming in contact with microaggressions and a weird culture. I felt like I didn't have support. And then my favorite teacher introduced me to some people from UC Berkeley who were doing some research. Apparently I wasn't the only one that knew that classes were low-key segregated. He explained to me the research that they were doing and also that there was an opportunity to make a change. That's where I got excited because, before, I didn't feel like I could do anything to make change.

He explained how we could put together a people of color support group for those who are going into classes and are the only Black kids and where people have a space to talk about microaggressions and get the support that we felt like we weren't getting. So that's what I did, and I felt like that was restorative, just having that space. It was a restorative space where we would sit in circles and talk about different things. But I wasn't formally introduced to restorative justice at that point, and I didn't know what it was.

Then that led to a bigger movement. The Oakland Unified School District sent some district officials to come and expand the pathway, and since I had already kind of done that work, I had the opportunity to lead in some of the district community conversations. That was really cool, and that was also restorative justice. But again, I still wasn't deep in it yet.

So I took what I learned from that. There was a book called *In Schools We Trust*, which talks about equity and education. I went to college and did politics, and we were having community discussions because we felt like a lot of the community wasn't aware of the different policies that were going on and that affected them. So I kept that restorative process with me, having circles and building community. But again, I still didn't know what it was in college.

Then I came back and worked for the county for a little bit. And after I left my county job, I didn't have a job for three or four months. RJOY has a men's group that meets at Lake Merritt every Thursday. So when I didn't have a job, I would just spend my time at the lake just planning, relaxing, or skating. A couple of times I went by, and I saw them and went, that's interesting. You don't usually see a circle of Black people talking. And then I would just keep skating. But this one time I skated for three hours or something. I was really hungry, and I saw them there. I'm like, man, they have some food, but I don't want to just eat food and dip, so I stayed. Then I attended their circles for like a year, and then they were like, you would be a good fit in the organization. I was like, okay. So that's how I got into it.

That's the best origin story.

Yeah, after I got formally trained in restorative justice, or at least how we train people, I was able to see that it's been a part of my life since high school—building community and conflict resolution and learning how to welcome people into community.

Why was participating in the high school group and in the Black men's circle so powerful for you?

I had a voice. And I had people to support me in high school. Like I said, I was frustrated because I felt like I wasn't getting support from my teachers or friends. I felt like I was not understood by people who didn't really understand the situation, and I didn't have the power to do anything about it. When I was able to join that club and start holding circles with people like that, I saw (1) that I wasn't the only one, and (2) that my voice and my experience matters, and then (3) that we could do something about it collectively by sharing our stories. And that was a more activist case—restorative justice righting a wrong that was done by policy.

The Black men's circle was a more personal case. We're not meeting together to fix anything per se but more so to fix us individually. At that time it was important because I had just [gone through] a breakup, and I felt like I couldn't trust any of my friends because it ended kind of messy. So I was like, man, I don't have anybody. I noticed that most of my friends were women. I'm only getting one side. I don't really have a lot of men that I can talk to, especially Black men. So it [the men's group] definitely filled a void. A lot of the people there were elders, and they were not afraid to talk about anything. So it was cool because I don't have that in my family. I have my dad and my uncle, but we just aren't open. So it was cool to have a space where I could talk about anything, and again, my voice was heard.

In the Black men's circle we talked about relationships, what it means to be a man, masculinity, [and] valuing yourself because you exist, and not necessarily because of the materials that you have. We had a lot of conversations.

Tell me more about your work at RJOY.

At RJOY, we use Ubuntu as a framework. *Ubuntu* is a Bantu word that means "I am because we are." The concept is that through dialogue and having conversations with people, you can see people in their humanity.

A lot of schools and people that we train are immediately interested in the conflict. But you have to have tier 1 first. You can't have conflict mediation if there's no trust, and a lot of that trust is built in community building. The goal is to build community first.

So, we train people. There's a youth program, and we have internships. Then we have circles throughout the week for different demographics, such as the Black men's circle (which is how I came to RJOY), the Black women's circle, Sista Cypher for women of color, and QTPOC for queer people of color and allies of color. Outside of those weekly circles, we do community healing. For example, there was beef in North Oakland between two families, and we brought them together to have a conversation so they could see each other and talk about their needs and everything.

We're also in schools as peacekeepers. When people say peacekeepers, they think of security guards. [It's] not really that, but people that the students can check in with. A lot of times, the teachers don't have the time or the availability to check in with students. When people do get the opportunity to check in with students, it's not always from a restorative mindset.

What advice would you give to teachers if they're interested in this work?

I would say that patience works. You need patience all throughout this work in several different contexts—patience with your own capabilities and patience with the people that you're working with that you want to be in your circle. Because honestly, it's really about working on your heart and also building relationships. And neither of those are immediate fixes. It takes a while to change and to want to change and to show up in an empathetic way and grow in a community mindset. It also takes time for people to be able to trust each other and want to be with each other so that those relationships can happen.

The focus is on building community, not necessarily just fixing problems. When you have a strong sense of community, people are naturally willing to lean into what is uncomfortable to solve those problems and come to a solution. But when people don't know each other or potentially have conflict with each other already and you're not working on that trust, then a lot of times it's a lot harder.

Can you speak to your thoughts about how this work can't just be in a vacuum, and how it has to be tied to equity and issues of racial equity?

I appreciate that you asked that because a lot of people will be like, what is restorative justice? And it's really hard to explain because it's not really one category, one field. It's like a frame of thinking. It's a worldview. And that's why it's able to fit into so many categories. There's several different components to it—there's racial justice, there's fighting mass incarceration, there's addressing misogyny and patriarchy. All of that ties in to restorative justice because in all those different systems of oppression, you aren't seeing people as people.

The goal of restorative justice is being able to see each other in [our] full humanity. Anything that stops you from that you have to lean into. Those are some of the topics that we try to lean into in our program. Each month we have a different theme. We have systemic racism, racial justice, food equity, and food justice. What I go over with the youth is a lot of times we see these inequities [like], say, the hood doesn't have any grocery stores, and we just think that's the way it is. But that is a consequence of food harm. It wasn't always like that. So, we go over food, equity, and different ways that you could solve inequities and on the personal level and at schools. All of that plays into restorative justice. The goal of restorative justice is to be able to see everybody in their full humanity, which includes their social and emotional energy, perceptions, and sense of self.

29

Making the Connection to Social-Emotional Learning

The Collaborative for Academic, Social, and Emotional Learning (CASEL) is widely considered one of the country's leading organizations dedicated to establishing evidenced-based social-emotional learning practices from preK through high school. In fact, CASEL coined the now ubiquitous term *social-emotional learning* in 1994. According to CASEL, SEL is

> *the process through which all young people and adults acquire and apply the knowledge, skills, and attitudes to develop healthy identities, manage emotions and achieve personal and collective goals, feel and show empathy for others, establish and maintain supportive relationships, and make responsible and caring decisions.* (2024c)

The five main SEL competencies, often referred to as the CASEL 5, are self-awareness, self-management, social awareness, relationship skills, and responsible decision-making.

These five competencies quite naturally overlap with the many skills that are developed via restorative practices and, in particular, personal narrative. In fact, CASEL released a guide in collaboration with partners at the International Institute for Restorative Practices (IIRP) that illustrates the alignment between SEL and restorative practices (Figure D-1).

Self-awareness		Self-management
The abilities to understand one's own emotions, thoughts, and values and how they influence behavior across contexts	Implementation of restorative practices in schools will help to build CASEL's five SEL competencies, including...	The abilities to manage one's emotions, thoughts, and behaviors effectively in different situations and to achieve goals and aspirations
Social awareness	**Relationship skills**	**Responsible decision-making**
The abilities to understand the perspectives of and empathize with others, including those from diverse backgrounds, cultures, and contexts	The abilities to establish and maintain healthy and supportive relationships to effectively navigate settings with diverse individuals and groups	The abilities to make caring and constructive choices about personal behavior and social interactions across diverse situations

FIGURE D-1: Aligning restorative practices and the CASEL SEL competencies for adults and students (adapted from CASEL, 2024a)

THE FIVE SEL COMPETENCIES

The first SEL competency, *self-awareness*, is our ability to process how we're feeling. It includes examining how our emotions, biases, and values may impact our behavior. Self-awareness also involves seeing our own strengths and weaknesses and developing a sense of self-confidence and purpose.

While self-awareness is all about understanding our emotions, *self-management* is all about what we *do* with those emotions. How do we monitor how our emotions and thoughts translate into our behavior? Self-management also includes developing strategies for managing stress and motivation, as well as setting personal goals and managing frustration and anger in relationships. The process of crafting personal narratives requires a great deal of both self-awareness and self-management, as crafting and sharing stories aims to equip learners to reflectively see themselves, their thought processes, emotions, and actions from an objective lens.

The competency of *responsible decision-making* involves our ability to make productive choices about our personal behavior and our interactions with others. This competency also includes thinking about the consequences of our actions, our ability to take into account ethics and safety, and our impact on a personal, interpersonal, collective, and institutional scale. This is also a key component of personal narrative and the Story of Self approach, which centers on the three-part formula of identifying a challenge, choice, and outcome. Crafting a story of self thus requires reflections on the outcomes of the decisions you've made. We will dive into a more detailed example of a story of self at the whole-school level in Chapter 31.

Next, the competency of *relationship skills* means that we can build, maintain, and navigate relationships with others. Not surprisingly, developing communication and cooperative skills is key in this arena. This competency also includes how we handle conflict in various social and cultural settings as well as how we seek out or offer help and support. When students form deep connections with their peers, they develop many different forms of relationships, ranging from romantic relationships to classroom peer relationships. During this process, they are navigating the many different stages of being in a relationship as well as the natural nuisances that are unforeseen to them. One of the stages is the situation where things get "dicey"—that is, where they're not seeing eye to eye with the other person. It is a natural part of being in a relationship and in life, but for a student, it can be extremely challenging to manage. Through these experiences of conflict, tension, disagreements, and the like, students will experience uneasiness and develop emotions that may be unfamiliar to them, leaving them confused about how to manage their emotions or how to react to the person they're upset with. The vast majority of the time, students react from a place of emotion.

Students attend school to learn social skills they will need in their immediate lives, in their future lives, and in between. One very important aspect of attending school is to learn how to make, maintain, and engage in collaborative relationships while effectively communicating with their counterparts and developing the skills to connect with their world.

Restorative practices cultivate and foster healthy ways of forging and maintaining relationships by making the competencies of social-emotional learning accessible. These competencies help everyone involved in the process develop a healthy identity, but most importantly, these experiences are fundamental building blocks for young adults. Through restorative circles, students learn how to empathize with others and take responsibility for their actions. Indigenous communities rely on restorative practices to ensure everyone's voice is on the same level and that there is no hierarchy in the circle. In the school environment, we are responsible not only for educating students, but also for teaching them skill sets and attributes that will lead them to be active and healthy members of society. Furthermore, restorative practices are a vehicle that empowers students and adults to coexist and collaborate in a thriving environment that fosters a safe and healthy community.

As part of their identity development, the student is entering a stage where it is vital to communicate, and doing so requires them to learn how to engage and interact with others verbally and nonverbally in a respectful way. Indigenous communities believe that it is a basic human right to be respected by others for one's innate and extrinsic attributes, persona, beliefs, values, physical qualities and limitations, emotional aura, and mental strengths and challenges. Thus, it is crucial to students' development of this skill set that the school teach them how to use respectful language (including body language) during interactions with adults and peers, as well as how to acquire academic language and when to use it. In fact, it is vital for schools to provide a space in the classroom where students can acquire and practice their communication skills. When the student is present in a restorative practice circle, they are essential and significant to others in the space. When the student is fully present, they are observing verbal and nonverbal signs that demonstrate how to communicate with and to others. Besides what is being said, the student is registering how things are being expressed, which includes but is not limited to eye contact, cadence, intonation, body language, body proximity, gestures, and posture.

Lastly, *social awareness* is the ability to understand the perspectives of others, including those who come from backgrounds or cultures that are different from our own. Social awareness also focuses on practicing empathy and compassion and the ability to understand social norms in a variety of settings.

Respecting multiple perspectives can be a significant challenge for students. Many students are not equipped to understand that others may have the same experience or see the same image but will have a completely different perspective than their own. When students share their individual perspectives, they believe that their truth is the *only* truth. A restorative practice circle allows them to be heard and to embrace, respect, and value the diversity of their peers and other members of the circle.

At the start of any restorative circle, members collectively create and agree on norms that will help guide and influence what follows. During sharing time, members support one another and hold each other accountable with the norms set forth. These experiences of hearing others and accepting their perspectives tie back to two of the CASEL competency skills: self-awareness and social awareness.

During the circle process, using a talking piece and having students respond to prompts in a clockwise direction helps instill patience. Sharing this space requires students to listen and process responses. When students are active listeners and participants in a restorative practice circle, they are learning that others are with them in the present and that they in turn are with others. They become aware of what others are saying, begin to understand and accept others' perspectives, and become more appreciative of their situation. Utilizing restorative circles in the classroom helps shape a culture of listening through giving attention to each other and saying just enough.

In essence, both SEL and restorative practices ultimately seek to build equitable learning environments and prioritize creating a sense of community and uplifting student voices (Figure D-2). With their focus on strengthening school climate vis-à-vis strengthening student–student and student–teacher relationships, both can also contribute to improved attendance and engagement, as well as to reductions in exclusionary discipline practices and disproportionality in discipline (CASEL, 2024a).

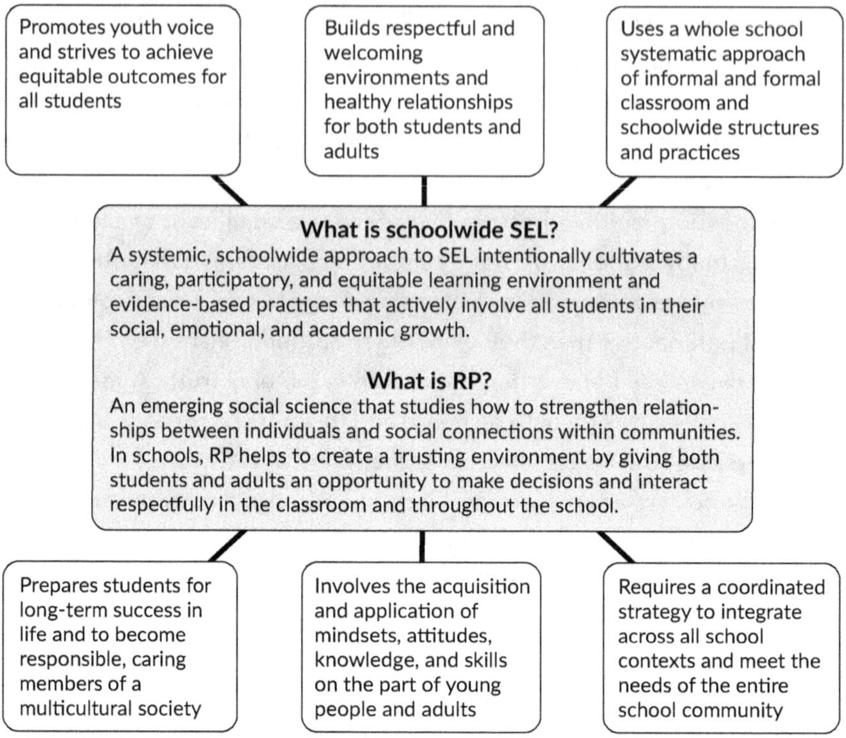

What is schoolwide SEL?
A systemic, schoolwide approach to SEL intentionally cultivates a caring, participatory, and equitable learning environment and evidence-based practices that actively involve all students in their social, emotional, and academic growth.

What is RP?
An emerging social science that studies how to strengthen relationships between individuals and social connections within communities. In schools, RP helps to create a trusting environment by giving both students and adults an opportunity to make decisions and interact respectfully in the classroom and throughout the school.

Surrounding boxes:
- Promotes youth voice and strives to achieve equitable outcomes for all students
- Builds respectful and welcoming environments and healthy relationships for both students and adults
- Uses a whole school systematic approach of informal and formal classroom and schoolwide structures and practices
- Prepares students for long-term success in life and to become responsible, caring members of a multicultural society
- Involves the acquisition and application of mindsets, attitudes, knowledge, and skills on the part of young people and adults
- Requires a coordinated strategy to integrate across all school contexts and meet the needs of the entire school community

FIGURE D-2: Common characteristics of SEL and RP (adapted from CASEL, 2024a)

THE AMYGDALA HIJACK

The importance of building a solid classroom environment is supported by Anderson's (2016) conditions of nurture, three elements that must be present in order for students to fully engage with their learning:

- **Safety:** Learners need to feel safe enough to take risks inherent in choice.
- **Inclusion:** Learners need to feel a positive connection to the class.
- **Collaboration:** Learners must be able to work with each other well.

Physical and emotional safety, a sense of belonging, and respectful communication with peers are all tenets of SEL and restorative practices.

If we put on our UDL hats again and think in terms of barriers, let's imagine what the opposite of these ideal conditions of nurture would look like. What might prevent a student from experiencing a sense of security in the classroom? What does that look like neurologically, and what are the effects of a threat to that security on a student's ability to learn?

One of those potential threats is an amygdala hijack, which, as mentioned in Chapter 22, is when the body's automatic fight, flight, or freeze mechanism is activated and stimulated and we lose the ability to think rationally. We all respond to perceived threats or danger by fighting (confronting the threat), fleeing (escaping the threat), or freezing (becoming immobile or passive), reactions triggered by the body's stress response system, which is centered in a part of the brain called the amygdala.

In an amygdala hijack, chemicals such as cortisol are released in our brain, limiting access to our neocortex and thus hindering our ability to think new thoughts and make new connections. It also cuts off access to long-term memory, so our ability to access funds of knowledge and prior information is gone. This effect can last for up to three hours, which means that our ability to learn can be fundamentally compromised for up to three hours.

Unfortunately, amygdala hijacks happen on a regular basis in our schools. As educators, we must be willing to acknowledge this and address it proactively. We can mitigate amygdala hijacks by creating predictable and safe environments with systems, structures, and routines that communicate and reinforce that we believe in our students.

We want to make sure our young people understand that their emotions and emotional energy are not something they should run away from. Those feelings, that emotional energy, helps communicate things about them, about their environment, and about what's going on. If we can help them develop the metacognitive ability to see and access this knowledge, they will be able to process and engage in internal and reflective questioning, such as: *Hey, when I feel a certain thing, why am I feeling this? Is this thing making me feel a certain way because I'm feeling anxiety or frustration? Does it have something to do with how I see myself?*

We soothe the amygdala by helping students understand their emotions, giving them options for breaks, and providing them with sentence stems. Essentially, we design learning and use restorative practices so that students will not be further triggered by participating in them.

We are not simply teaching content for the sake of content. We are showing our students how to develop agency and self-efficacy; we are teaching them about how they learn and how to advocate for themselves and what they need. This is reinforced through centering student voice, and reflection in particular, in a manner that includes not only exploration of identity and journey but also feeling and emotion. Developing social-emotional learning and awareness is central to restorative practice work. Our learners need to be aware of their feelings and what those feelings mean so that they can make appropriate decisions that will support the best outcome both for themselves and for others.

We normalize this awareness by asking students to share not only their thoughts but also their feelings about content, assignments, situations, and circumstances. For example, when unpacking a learning target or objective, ask, "What do you think this means? Why do you think we're doing this, and how do you feel about it?" We want our learners to be aware of what is being required of them or what they will be learning about, as well as aware of their own reactions to that. Are they feeling excited, frustrated, angry, apathetic, or anxious?

As our learners become aware of their emotional energy and are able to make appropriate decisions and choices based on that information, they're building metacognition. Consider this reflective response: "This objective makes me anxious. I don't feel confident about my ability to do this, and some members of this class made fun of me and made me feel dumber the last time we did something like this. I think I need to check in with you and that I need extra time. I also need to not work with Jamal or Charles because I'll be off task and embarrassed if they see me struggling with it." This shows that the learner is self-aware, mindful of their emotional energy, in touch with what these emotions mean, and choosing a course of action that takes all this information into consideration so that they can achieve success in the lesson.

Also consider implementing CASEL's three signature practices, which are dynamic pedagogical tools to help soothe students' amygdalas. The SEL 3, as they are commonly known, are the inclusive welcome, engaging strategies, and the intentional close and can be used as follows (CASEL, 2024b):

1. Begin each class period, meeting, or learning experience with an *inclusive welcome*—an activity, routine, or ritual that builds community and connects to the work ahead. Some examples:
   - Smile warmly and greet each person by their preferred name.
   - Implement whole-group greeting activities.
   - Hold morning circles.
   - Provide interactive "do-nows," such as peer-to-peer homework help.

2. Embed *engaging strategies*, such as brain breaks to anchor thinking and learning, throughout the experience. Engaging strategies offer many opportunities of varying complexity to practice SEL skills. Choosing intentional strategies and activities with sequenced steps that suit your group's current needs promotes engagement and supports learning both individually (e.g., "turn and talk" with a partner) and collectively (e.g., Socratic seminar and Jigsaw activities). Build in a balance of interactive and reflective experiences to meet the needs of all participants. Additional examples of engaging strategies include:
   - **Think, Ink, Pair, Share:** Give students silent time to reflect, write, and work in partners, and then close with a group share-out.
   - **Clock Partners:** Prearrange partners for quickly pairing up for reflection and discussion.
   - **Private Think-Time:** Provide participants with time to process and reflect before moving forward.
   - **Mindful Minute Brain Break:** Use short breaks to promote focus and readiness to learn.

3. An *intentional close* means concluding each learning experience with intention. This can highlight individual and shared understanding of the importance of the work, provide a sense of accomplishment, and

support forward thinking. The closing activity may reflect the learning, help identify next steps, or make connections to one's own work. Here are some sentence stems for intentional closes:

- Something I learned today . . .
- I am curious about . . .
- I am looking forward to tomorrow because . . .
- Something I still question . . .
- Something that still concerns me . . .

We must equip learners with strategies that enable them to practice self-awareness. Students should have options available when they realize they've been triggered or feel emotional energy that would otherwise cause them to respond inappropriately or lead to an outcome they do not want. Proactively having these strategies in place also reinforces the belief that our learners have the capacity to make decisions that will be in everyone's best interest.

30

The S.O.D.A. Strategy

One of our favorite strategies is the S.O.D.A. strategy (Table D-1), from Zaretta Hammond's *Culturally Responsive Teaching and the Brain* (2015), which stands for stop, observe, detach, and awaken. Mirko and Pam personally utilized this strategy for regulating emotions while at the Putnam Avenue Upper School. Our commitment to modeling the practices, climate, and culture that we wished to see students emulate meant that we all practiced and modeled what using this strategy looked like in action. Many staff members posted copies of this strategy near their desks, and we had student copies posted in classrooms and the hallways.

In the next chapter, Dr. Christina Farese, the instructional coach during our time together at the Putnam Avenue Upper School, shares some examples of how the use of personal narrative and the Story of Self approach were essential healing tools for our school community.

TABLE D-1: THE S.O.D.A. STRATEGY: Steps to Gain Control of Your Emotions (Adapted From Hammond, 2015)

STEPS	HOW? WHY?
Stop	Take a moment to stop and pause before reacting the way you usually would. When you step into a situation that feels challenging, push yourself to stay open-minded. Being open-minded means staying open to perspectives other than your own. That might look like not letting a student's animated verbal exchange—or any other cultural expression—throw you off or trigger a reaction.
Observe	Check yourself before reacting. Pause and take a breath. Give yourself 10 seconds—that's about how long it takes for stress hormones to travel through your body and hit your prefrontal cortex. In those first moments, cortisol and adrenaline are starting to kick in, but you still have some "wiggle room" to lean on your wiser self. This is your chance to interrupt the amygdala from taking over by using stress management techniques. Try describing what's happening to yourself in neutral terms. This step is key—it's where you can realize that what you first saw as a threat might not actually be real.
Detach	Sometimes when we get triggered, we get caught up in needing to be right or trying to assert control over others. When that happens, intentionally shift your focus to something positive or inspiring. If that doesn't work, grab a drink of water or take a few steps back—literally move yourself to reset your energy. When we let go of the need to be right or defend ourselves, we can channel that energy into responding thoughtfully instead of reacting impulsively.
Awaken	When your amygdala kicks in, it's just trying to protect you. But shifting your focus from yourself to the person in front of you can help you snap out of it and stay present. Remind yourself that they're a person with their own feelings—they might even be scared and reacting out of fear. Ask yourself a few quick questions: What might they be thinking? How could they be feeling right now? Taking a moment to see things from their perspective can pull you out of reactive mode and put you in a better space to have a more productive, positive interaction.

31

Story of Self: Honoring Students' Identities and Social-Emotional Learning

DR. CHRISTINA FARESE

In 1994, scholar Herbert Kohl wrote, "To agree to learn from a stranger who does not respect your integrity causes a major loss of self. The only alternative is to not-learn." This statement was as true in 1994 as it is now. Nowhere is relationship more important than during the middle school years, which are a linchpin for students in terms of identity development and academic trajectory. The collective work of Zaretta Hammond, Dr. Christopher Emdin, Dr. Beverly Tatum, Dr. Sara Lawrence-Lightfoot, and Herbert Kohl highlights the connection among honoring the identities of the students in front of us, relationships, and learning. Students actively disengage and choose to not-learn when there is a lack of relationship. But, often in schools, how to put that knowledge into practice becomes a multilayered challenge—and one that results in alienation and active not-learning.

At the Putnam Avenue Upper School, a Grade 6–8 school in the Cambridge Public School District serving approximately 270 students, we worked diligently to put our students on track for the "Good Life"—the best quality of life as students defined it for themselves. We employed Story of Self, derived from Marshall Ganz's framework of public narrative, as a key lever for bridging the gap between theory and practice. For us, Story of Self was an opportunity for everyone in our community to demonstrate our core value of pride in our identities and to reflect on a challenge, a choice, and the outcome in our lives. This process became a cornerstone of our advisory program and the entry point for building relationships and creating a school culture where students' identities were honored.

Story of Self is part of a larger framework developed by activist, political organizer, and Harvard professor Marshall Ganz. It is founded on the idea that "stories not only teach us how to act—they inspire us to act. Stories communicate our values through the language of the heart, our emotions. And it is what we feel—our hopes, our cares, our obligations—not simply what we know that can inspire us with the courage to act" (Ganz, 2011). Story of Self asks individuals to consider their values and frame a story from their experience that highlights a choice, a challenge, and an outcome. Stories of self are framed around a challenge, a choice, and an outcome because "by telling our personal stories of challenges we have faced, choices we have made, and what we learned from the outcomes we can inspire others and share our own wisdom. Because stories allow us to express our values not as abstract principles, but as lived experience, they have the power to move others" (Ganz, 2011). Overall, Story of Self stands on the importance of public narrative in our own lives, our community, and our world.

WHAT IS A SUCCESSFUL STORY OF SELF?

At Putnam Ave., we identified and adapted three criteria from Ganz's work to highlight what would constitute a successful story of self:

- A good public narrative is drawn from the series of choice points that have structured the "plot" of your life—the challenges you've faced, choices you've made, and outcomes you've experienced.

- The power in your story of self is to reveal something of yourself and your values—not your deepest secrets, but the key shaping moments in your life.
- Your story models authentic fragility and honesty.

From these criteria, we developed a single-point rubric (see Figure D-3) to use with staff and students that considered how the story of self was presented as well.

PAUS Story of Self Rubric

CONTENT

Feedback for Growth	Criteria	Evidence of Exceeding the Criteria
	A good public narrative is drawn from the series of choice points that have structured the "plot" of your life – the challenges you faced, choices you made, and outcomes you experienced.	
	The power in your story of self is to reveal something of yourself and your values—not your deepest secrets, but the key shaping moments in your life.	
	Models authentic fragility and honesty.	

DELIVERY

Feedback for Growth	Criteria	Evidence of Exceeding the Criteria
	The organization, development, vocabulary, and style are appropriate to task, purpose, and audience.	
	• Maintains appropriate eye contact, adequate volume and speed, and clear pronunciation • Rarely uses filler words (ahh, umm, etc.)	
	• Holds the attention of the audience and demonstrates enthusiasm for the content • Uses natural gestures and movements	

FIGURE D-3: Single-point rubric

We consciously decided to use a single-point rubric due to its simplicity, as well as the opportunity to present feedback to students that was specific both about areas of growth and areas of excellence and that was criteria-based (Gonzalez, 2017). Feedback—from peers, from teachers, from themselves—is an essential part of telling and sharing a story.

Additionally, what we say and how we provide feedback to students matters, and it matters even more to our students of color—particularly when that feedback is coming from a White teacher. Honest appraisals of student work against specific criteria for success and within a context of support (Cohen & Steele, 2002) are essential for students who face stereotype threat, microaggressions, and racism on a daily basis. This process of sharing, providing feedback, and revising builds and/or deepens relationships, especially if it is done with respect, attention to clear criteria, and in consideration of areas of both strength and growth.

HOW DID STORY OF SELF WORK AT PUTNAM AVENUE?

At Putnam Ave., advisory was a daily time that we spent in small groups building relationships with students, supporting social-emotional learning, and working toward a common goal. Our theory of action was:

If we **build relationships** with students **by**:

- exploring and honoring their identities (story of self),
- reflecting on their progress with the core values (portfolio),
- assisting with executive function (school-wide organization system), and
- celebrating reading (independent reading time and celebration),

then we will create a community where students are academically and socially successful. We believed that through these activities, relationships are built and nurtured; students will feel respected and their identities honored; their social-emotional skills will be further developed and practiced; and, as a result of all of this, students will become academically and socially successful. To that end, our advisory program comprised the story of self, circle practice, executive function support, a portfolio, and independent reading—all of which were also grounded in our core values and research, which made the following clear:

- Adolescents, particularly middle schoolers, need time to explore and think about their identity and need teachers who both recognize and embrace this (Tatum, 1997).

- The brain is social by nature and relationships are a precursor for learning. When the brain feels unsafe, it cannot learn, and culture is a key element of this (Hammond, 2015).

- Stories are important both for communicating our beliefs and for building relationships that enable us to work together (Ganz, 2009).

During advisory—from the first week through the first few months of school—staff and students spent time crafting, practicing, and sharing their stories of self. All of this work together created an experience where staff and students could reflect, embrace the personal power of framing and telling their own story, form deep connections, and exhibit our core value: "We take pride in our identities and the impact we have on both individuals and larger society. We think not only about the here and now, but about the future as well, considering carefully how each choice we make will impact the future of our own lives as individuals and the future of our collective community." Students and staff had multiple opportunities to practice and revise their stories before the school-wide Story of Self Day, generally held in December, and attended by members of the community.

It is essential to note that this did not happen all in one year. Our work began in August of 2017 when we introduced Story of Self to the staff by modeling it as an administrative team. Then, in staff meetings and common planning times during the early part of the 2017–18 school year, staff were provided with organizers and time to craft their own story of self, as well as to participate in simulations that modeled how to work on Story of Self with students in advisory. All of this work drafting, revising, and practicing culminated for teachers in a staff meeting where they presented their stories to one another. Then, this work was replicated in advisories with our students, also culminating in a day where sixth graders presented to their advisories and seventh and eighth graders presented to their advisories and families. As we grew and learned more in the subsequent school year, we included a public, school-wide presentation day, as mentioned above. See Table D-2 for a sample advisory lesson plan.

TABLE D-2: Putnam Avenue Upper School Demo Advisory: Story of Self

TIME	ACTIVITY
6 min.	**Listen** to an example of a story: https://player.themoth.org/#/?actionType=ADD_AND_PLAY&storyid=392
6 min.	**Discuss** (select based on students): • What did you think of the story? Did you enjoy it? What makes you say that? • What did you notice about how the speaker told the story? • Challenge, choice, outcome. Did you notice these? What were they? Did they help the story? • How did the speaker model fragility or honesty? • What did the story reveal about the speaker's values?
3 min.	**Circle share:** If you were writing your own story of self, what do you definitely want to include?

At our inaugural Story of Self Day, we had almost 200 visitors—ranging from members of the superintendent's cabinet to school committee members, local university faculty, DESE staff, parents of rising fifth graders, Putnam Ave. families, community partners, and a record company CEO—all of whom celebrated with us the courage of our amazing students as they shared their personal narratives. This experience spotlighted how focused, brave, poised, respectful, and courageous our students are. Our students proved that they could maintain a safe and brave space as they treated one another with respect, dignity, and confidentiality throughout the entirety of this process and supported one another in being publicly vulnerable. They were deeply respectful of one another's stories, our guests, and our school community. Survey data collected after the Story of Self Day showed that 78% of students found the process of writing their story of self enjoyable and fulfilling; 75% of students felt empowered by sharing their story of self; and, 66% of students felt that they had learned something about themselves from sharing their story.

HOW DOES STORY OF SELF EXTEND BEYOND THE CLASSROOM?

To be clear, Story of Self, while a linchpin of our advisory program, was only one element among many aimed at enabling students and staff to share who they are and to center students' voices in the learning environment. Story of Self provides an opportunity to frame your own experience and to be vulnerable in a safe environment—and it was modeled throughout the community, from the administrative team to the students. Ultimately, choosing the framing for your experience and sharing something of yourself leads to empowerment. When students feel empowered and respected—which results from the powerful connections that form when administrators, teachers, and students share their stories with one another—they are able to learn. Our advisory program, in conjunction with our emphasis on UDL and restorative practices, resulted in decreases in office referrals and suspensions as well as increases in student growth and achievement percentile. Story of Self was the connective thread that not only set the stage for learning but also provided a springboard for the relationships at the heart of learning.

32

Pause and Reflect On Part D

SUMMARY

The foundations of social-emotional learning (SEL), commonly known as the CASEL 5—self-awareness, self-management, social awareness, relationship skills, and responsible decision-making—are integral to building a transformative educational journey. These SEL competencies, closely intertwined with the principles of restorative practices, cultivate an educational landscape enriched with empathy, collaboration, and personal growth. The alignment between SEL and restorative practices fosters the development of students' emotional intelligence and relational abilities. Both SEL and restorative practices create an equitable and thriving learning environment founded on inclusivity, respect, and collaboration.

REFLECTION QUESTIONS

1. How can the alignment of SEL and restorative practices shape a more inclusive and empathetic classroom environment?

2. How can you integrate welcoming activities, engaging strategies, and optimistic closures to foster emotional well-being and connection?

3. How might the practice of observing and describing emotions during an amygdala hijack empower students to regain control of their responses?

4. How does the infusion of SEL competencies into classroom dynamics nurture empathy and understanding among students from diverse backgrounds?

5. In what ways can educators promote a shift from reactive to responsive behavior through fostering social awareness and emotional intelligence?

6. How can educators design learning experiences that allow students to explore and articulate their emotions, leading to greater self-awareness and self-efficacy?

7. How might the incorporation of restorative practices into classroom routines enhance students' ability to manage emotions, resolve conflicts, and engage in productive relationships?

8. How does the convergence of SEL, restorative practices, and UDL empower students to become more active in their own emotional growth and development?

PART E

Change Isn't One-Size-Fits-All

I am, because we are, and since we are, therefore I am.
—J.S. Mbiti, Kenyan-born theologian and author

33

The Purpose of School Change: Healing and Restoration

Change takes time. As educators, when we are faced with crisis after crisis and need some kind of lifeline, hearing that change takes time is probably the last thing we want to hear but also the first thing we need to remember. How long does change take? For school culture, the research says three to five years (Gruenert & Whitaker, 2017).

Let's take a step back, though, and first examine the type of change we're talking about. Are we thinking of something more technical that needs to be fixed, such as finding new school scheduling software? Or are we thinking of something a little more intangible, such as wanting to build or improve a culture of collaboration among our teachers? According to Heifetz and Linsky (2002), there are two types of challenges: technical and adaptive. Technical challenges can be solved by applying "existing know-how" and employing various problem-solving processes (2002). If your school is facing issues with scheduling and there's a new software program that can fix it, figure out how to purchase it, who to train, and when to roll it out. Boom! That's a relatively easy fix that can have concrete deliverables and a timeline. Adaptive challenges, on the other hand, require the people within an organization to change their ways; if the people are the issue, the solution lies with them. As Heifetz and Linsky write, "Without learning new ways—changing attitudes, values, and behaviors—people cannot make the adaptive leap necessary to thrive in the new environment" (2002, p. 13).

Adaptive challenges by their very definition cannot have a quick fix. When we rush to impose a technical fix on an adaptive challenge, that initiative is doomed to fail, and we risk undermining or sabotaging the very initiatives we hoped to roll out. When things don't work, it's easy for us or our staff to blame the initiative versus the implementation. In terms of restorative practices, too often, administrators or staff might have some initial zeal about bringing restorative practices to their school—by, say, rushing to teach staff how to run a harm circle—without fully understanding that these practices are at their core a commitment to a belief system. When this happens, inevitably those hasty or ill-conceived measures won't achieve the outcomes everyone was hoping for. Unfortunately, instead of reflecting on how these programs were rolled out, some may come to the immediate conclusion that restorative practices simply don't work.

People sometimes say that teaching is an art, not a science, and that statement is usually a response to some conversation in which one individual seems to want a cookie-cutter, silver-bullet solution to a complex issue. Similarly, when we think of school change and restorative practices, there are, of course, end goals and signposts that we can follow, but we also need to allow room for each school's unique wants and needs. While our unwavering goal as educators and restorative practices practitioners should be on building community and promoting healing, and while there are overall steps and strategies for achieving successful implementation, we must keep in mind that just as no two students are alike, no two schools are alike. Mirko and Pam's school and Edgar's school are not the only ones who have wrestled with this work and experienced success. Educators all across the world and nation are grappling with the need for healing in their communities and are using these tools and mindsets to get there.

With this in mind, let's hear from a practitioner who balanced the unique needs of his school community while still standing firm in his belief in the power of healing and relationships. Jamel Adkins-Sharif, EdD, JD, one of Mirko and Pam's former colleagues in Cambridge, Massachusetts, led restorative practices initiatives at an elementary school he ran in Boston. He writes in the next chapter about how shifting mindsets was one of the keys to bringing about changes in his school's culture. This form of adaptive change manifested in Dr. Sharif's efforts to emphasize the importance of reclaiming marginalized identities and histories, actions that are not merely technical fixes but involve changing hearts and minds.

34

Decolonizing Education, Shifting Mindsets

JAMEL ADKINS-SHARIF, EDD, JD

I didn't have the answers or all the language for what I was trying in my last principalship. All I knew was I ran the Blackstone Innovation School, an elementary school in Boston that seemed out of control, and I was expected to do something about it. There was a rash of first and second graders who fought and bit children and teachers and often bolted from class. There were overwhelmed parents who needed help and others who wanted their kids kept safe from the mayhem. And there were teachers, some ready to bring down the hammer, others ready to quit, all expecting me to somehow right the ship so that they could focus on teaching and learning.

    This is not a happily-ever-after tale of the superhero principal, throwing the impossible on her back and flying off into exemplary sunsets. This is a story of what's possible when a school community comes to believe in the capacity for change, and individuals do their part to restore their own greatness. I will share leadership moves that aimed to create space for vulnerability, power sharing, and communicating care in the service of better learning environments for students and teachers. Restorative practices and culture can begin to take hold in a school when its stakeholders shift their mindsets about problem-solving. The first step in this shift is reflexivity and space for safe conversation.

PEACEMAKING CIRCLES

When conflict takes place, the impact goes far beyond direct parties. A child acting out in a classroom—say, breaking or throwing something or hitting someone—creates anxiety and fear among witnessing students. When routine, it creates in students' minds uncertainty about the safety of the class and their teacher's ability to keep them safe. The teacher may become hypervigilant in an effort to head trouble off, resulting in a shorter tolerance for typical behaviors, and may then start relying on punitive measures to establish control. All this gets communicated to families, giving them the sense (justified or otherwise) that their children are in daily peril at school. It can snowball into a self-fulfilling prophecy, with leaders constantly having to reassure caregivers who believe from personal experience and the "grapevine" that things are deteriorating. I have seen this cause an unhealthy and reactive class and school climate, seeing as how safety is an essential concern in elementary settings.

One approach to this challenge is to establish peacemaking circles. Use these circles when there is a recent conflict or an incident that needs processing or airing. In order to run circles effectively, the facilitator must be trained in restorative practices; you cannot simply stick a dean or assistant principal in this role, as it will be difficult to overcome the perception of their disciplinary function in an environment of respectful sharing. A peacemaking circle works well with elementary students when it is modeled and practiced often. It can't be introduced after a particularly difficult incident when students have had no previous experience solving problems this way. I didn't necessarily convince all staff to agree with restorative practices as a replacement for traditional approaches to behavior management, but they were willing to learn more and try it as one option. And the practice resonated with a cultural value of the school, articulated as Ubuntu—a South African term meaning "I am because we are." Through rituals associated with living Ubuntu, such as school chants and class performances, we emphasized the connection between the individual's and the collective's well-being.

COMMUNITY MORNING CIRCLES

Another form of circle centered on affirmations and envisioning a successful day with minimal conflict and the practice of de-escalation strategies. This was a strategy I brought to my leadership team to address six students, three each from Grades 1 and 2, who came to school dysregulated every day and whose day often spiraled into unproductivity as a result of some internal or external stressor. The constant attention to their extreme behaviors—the result of trauma both inside and outside of school—was wearing down their teachers as well as the student support team members sent to de-escalate or escort them from class. It seemed radical to some, but the idea was simple: What would it be like if these students began school by participating in circles in the gym with adults in the building and a few parents they had good relationships with and doing things most kids didn't do to start their day? What would it be like to show our most challenging students love and attention every morning from 8:10 to 8:30 a.m.? That was literally the question I posed in a meeting one morning, using de Bono's Six Thinking Hats protocols (1985) to promote broad thinking on possible responses. Those six babies would dance, sing, stretch, eat breakfast, and wrap up with an affirmation on how they wanted their day to go. On Fridays they could play math video games too. These daily moments began and ended in a circle and were filled with affirmations, some of which we said, drew, or danced. We would then escort those students to class. These efforts sometimes produced great results, where students began to self-regulate more or seek help when stressed rather than behave unsafely. For other children it was more incremental, often feeling like for every two steps forward, they took one step back. Still others had such significant issues that any positive impact was fleeting, and we needed to access mental health services.

All along as a leader, you have to convince folks the payoff is worth the effort, that even in failures and missteps there's learning and growth. As difficult as all of this is, was, and can be, it was tempered by the knowledge that (1) we now had data showing that we were making a difference for some students, which should be a measure of success, and (2) wanting something more than what we'd always done and taking new approaches to peace and community building could shift our view of what is possible. That's a result in and of itself.

INDIVIDUAL COUNSEL

A final practice I worked to implement in support of restorative practices was space for individual counsel and bidirectional feedback. In some ways, the other practices never really take root until this is established culture. This practice meant creating time and opportunity to listen extensively, build relationships, and seek clarity through asking questions. I attempted this with students, caregivers, and educators in order to normalize the process of reflection and clarity seeking with one another. I was hoping it'd help us make better decisions and consequently treat each other better.

Three things are required of a school leader for this practice to be effective. You must model vulnerability; you must seek to understand and not judge; and you must be willing to concede power and be on equal footing with anyone. At this elementary school, those were often the most difficult things to ask of others, so modeling meant living on that deserted island, self-doubt whispering all around. It meant sharing with that angry parent that you really didn't have an answer but you knew it wouldn't be found at each other's throats. It meant showing softness to the teacher who felt he was failing in both his parental and teaching obligations, recalling when you felt the same way. It meant sitting with the eight-year-old who keeps telling inappropriate jokes and giggling, waiting to see if I really wouldn't get mad in this meeting, wanting to know if it's safe to lower the class clown shield and kick it for real. It meant sharing your own vision and limitations as the leader and wondering aloud what others thought about it all. These moments must become routine, part of how you lead, debrief, inquire, and make meaning of the school and your place in it. In doing so, you draw from ancient knowledge, from established ways of calibrating and recentering yourself and your relationships with others.

As First Peoples—Africans and Indigenous peoples and their descendants—we universally designed, meaning we made broadly available to all, ways to be in community with each other, resolve conflict, and solve challenges through discourses about ourselves and our relation to creation and the divine. Current education and leadership praxis demands that African and Indigenous peoples reach back in order to move forward. We cannot forget that for millennia, we created learning institutions and practices that worked for our children and our societies. Implementing restorative practices in schools moves them closer to liberatory space and further from colonial designs over minds and bodies. Decolonizing education centrally involves the reclamation of our practices and ways of being, how we taught and loved our youth, the knowledge we relied upon, and the ways we held space and each other to account.

35

Magic Happens, but It's Not a Magic Wand

If restorative practices and UDL have taught us anything, it's that the power of collective voice and hearing from a multiplicity of voices is essential. In that spirit, we next present an interview with David Yusem, the restorative justice coordinator for the Oakland Unified School District (OUSD). An effort to bring about adaptive change at the district level, the OUSD restorative justice program began with one school in 2006 and has since expanded to approximately 30 schools in the district, with countless others making use of the district's RJ services.

David's personal commitment to the firm goal of community healing is evident throughout his career, but he implemented a variety of measures that worked for his particular context. In this conversation, you will see how the program has succeeded in part because the need for healing originated from the community itself rather than from the top down (the approach often taken with school initiatives). In addition, David emphasizes that restorative practices are about embracing a philosophy rather than a curriculum. He reminds us that social and racial justice must be at the root of restorative practices, and he doesn't shy away from recognizing that this work, while worthwhile and powerful, takes commitment and time.

(This transcribed interview has been edited for clarity and length.)

Tell us about yourself! How did you become involved in restorative justice work?

My background is in conflict resolution, and for the past 23 years or so, I've been engaged in community mediation. Eventually, long story short, I became the program manager for community mediation at a mediation service in the Bay Area that served Alameda County, which is Oakland. I was managing that work and doing trainings and facilitation but mostly working with volunteers and helping people work through conflict—all kinds of people in the community, all kinds of conflict. That's what I did for a long time. Then in 2007, I started hearing about restorative justice in Oakland through connecting with Restorative Justice for Oakland Youth (RJOY), who actually got their initial training through Roca, a Boston-based organization. [Roca is a nonprofit that addresses urban violence and engages youth and police in relationships.]

RJOY was just starting out at the time. I connected with them primarily through Fania Davis, who was one of the initial founders. She's Angela Davis's sister, and she's got a connection to the Black Panthers. They both live here in Oakland. The RJ work in Oakland became a logical next step in the work that the Black Panthers were doing, very much connected to their legacy in Oakland. That work, as Fania would say, is the *healing* version of that work—the warrior and the healer, as she puts it. Because I was doing conflict resolution and had the platform to begin to do this, I just started doing it at SEEDS [a nonprofit focused on conflict resolution] and practicing it, and being trained in it, and helping groups of people do circles. I then began to build pilot programs for this organization and was able to get restorative justice as one of the things that they did. I also started working at Alameda County Juvenile Hall and at Berkeley Unified School District and then at Oakland Unified as a thought partner as they began to implement it at OUSD.

Then in 2011, OUSD got some resources to hire a program manager to begin implementing RJ across the district. I got that job, and I've been there ever since. May 30th will be 13 years that I've been here, building a program, training people across the district, and doing our best to effect a culture shift across the school district with all the adults and the young people in the community and in the ecosystem. That's the short version of how I got into it and how I landed where I am now.

Was it difficult for the school district to understand the importance of this work?

It was just that the time had come. There was a lot of support from the community, and it moved from the community into the district as the legacy of the work the Black Panthers were doing. It wasn't like the superintendent heard about it at a conference and said, We're doing this, people. It was much more organic. One of the reasons why it's been so sustainable is because of how it came in, and how we've managed to maintain it and be consistent with it.

The biggest reason is because our big focus has been trying to get people to embrace a philosophy rather than a curriculum and a way of being with each other in community, and then using that as the foundation for everything else, including difficult conversations. That's very different from anything else that's ever been done in this whole district, so it's a big lift. But I do think that's one of the reasons why people don't know how to dispense with it. Because it's not something like a binder that they can just put on the shelf and say, Well, we're done with this; let's go on to the next thing. It's more like this philosophy, and if it takes hold, then it's there, and there's no way to get rid of it. But it does take constant vigilance to maintain it so that it doesn't drift into something else, which is easy for it to do.

Could you share an example of the work where you felt, this is what keeps me going?

There's so many moving examples. Generally speaking, community-building circles are just really nice to be in, and usually spaces of connection. To see a staff be able to connect with each other or students being able to connect with each other in that way is a really beautiful thing. I've been in tons of those where you do a circle just to connect, and it can be something silly you're talking about, or even playing games. We play a ton of games and do a lot of movement, somatic-type stuff. And that's really helpful to play. We're believers in play and being silly, and that's helpful.

But there's been some powerful circles around harm and conflict. One in particular was relayed to me by one of our RJ staff at a middle school. There was a shrine that some parents of a soldier who died in Iraq had put up in the community outside the school in the neighborhood, and a couple of students after school one day had destroyed the shrine. They quickly figured out who it was, and the [soldier's] parents had come to the school and said, hey, we're pretty sure some students did this, and they were devastated, of course. The school didn't suspend those students. What they did was, they prepped them, and the two parents agreed. They basically talked with all the impacted parties, the boys, their parents, the people whose shrine was destroyed, and they came together in a circle to talk about what happened. At one point, the woman whose son the shrine was for pulled out a picture of her son. She gave the picture to one of the boys and said, "You remind me of my son. I want you to have this picture of him." They talked about what happened and the impact. The students came by and helped them rebuild the shrine. And then a couple of weeks later, the boys came by and helped them prune trees and played some basketball in their driveway. They talked about what happened and the impact of that situation, all without needing to be suspended, and really [understood] the impact of what happened. So that kind of transformation is an example of a beautiful story, and it also speaks to the type of community that you can build using RJ as a community-building process rather than just a response to harm. If you just use it as a response to harm, then it's just going to be another punitive thing.

Is there an example where things didn't go as expected, and can you talk about why you thought that was?

Those examples happen all the time. I mean, I can't tell you how many circles.... I think that's just part of the process of the culture shift. I have a very high tolerance for stuff just going off the rails and not working. It happens all the time; I'm so used to it. I think the most recent time was with some students. We have a really great peer restorative justice program where every year, we train hundreds of students across our district to be circle keepers and understand RJ. And they love it, and they embrace it in a way that adults don't—more fidelity, better integrity—and they demand it as they move up in grades.

But in one of our middle schools, one of our RJ facilitators had to take leave, so I came in because of the students who are about to start doing circles in classrooms. And so I came in as someone who didn't know any of the students or any of the other classrooms or any of the teachers or anybody in the school. I came in to help the students do the circles. One circle I did was with a teacher who was brand new. The students in that class didn't even know her, and she had done no community building whatsoever. So when we were in there, the students were just going crazy. They did not in good faith participate in that circle, and the student who was leading the circle—I was just there supporting him—he just kept looking at me like, *What should we do?* We were in a circle, but nobody really cared in there.

That thing happens all the time. I tell people when we train them, just expect it to go wrong at first, and persevere. Have some patience. Keep going. Once people understand what it is, they will want it.

What are some of the challenges that come with shifting belief systems?

At first there was some resistance, a little bit here and there. I think we've crossed that bridge, so we don't really get much resistance. The biggest challenge now is just training as many people as need to be trained. And one of our biggest challenges is just money. Our model costs money. We don't just have volunteers from school sites form a team and try to do it. We actually created positions that are full-time, unionized positions at school sites called RJ facilitators. We used to have four RJ program managers that work with me. I'm the coordinator. So we used to have a pretty robust team, four program managers and myself, five of us essentially, that would then support all the RJ facilitators at the school site. That all costs money. In 2019, the district eliminated our budget because of a budget crisis that we were going through. So now it's just me and one other program manager, and then the site-based RJ staff are all supported by school site money instead of money my department used to have to help fund that position.

One of the challenges that goes along with that is that we're used to going to the experts when we need support with something, and the RJ model is different. We put someone in the school. Their job is to de-professionalize themselves so that they're supporting. They train and support everyone else in doing the work. So one of the challenges is that they become seen as "the RJ person," and you go to the RJ person for everything RJ-related rather than, how can that person support *me* in doing this? Some schools get it, some schools don't. It's just another example of how different RJ is, and how we need to shift our way of thinking about even things like that.

We live in a culture that's filled with violence and misogyny and poverty and all those big factors that play into what our schools look like. RJ is not a panacea. Yet all that impacts our work, and so doing something like restorative justice in an environment that's homeostatic is really difficult at times. It does take constant vigilance and being relentless in terms of our training and our coaching supports, modeling what we want to see, and trying to support the shifting of more punitive practices, even across the central office. So yeah, a lot of challenges.

Can you share examples of when RJ wasn't done with fidelity, or people meant well, but for whatever reason, it wasn't where it could have been in practice?

It needs to be done on a regular basis in a predictable way, which is a trauma-informed practice, but also as a ritual, so people will embrace it, especially if it's fun or you get to connect, and people love to feel connected. It just takes time to get there, so it doesn't really bother me when stuff goes off the rails. It just doesn't. That's part of working in a school, right? And then we've had times where people have said they are doing RJ—maybe they read about it somewhere or whatever—and then they bring people together where there's been harm, and they just do it wrong. They don't do prep ahead of time, which is absolutely crucial. They bring them together. Things go crazy. They create more harm. And that happens when you have a district of 36,000 students and thousands of staff, you're going to get people that are like, Oh, I know about RJ; sure, I'll do it. And they cause more harm. And that happens, too.

How does this work tie into issues of social justice and equity?

When I do trainings with some teachers about restorative practices, everyone's just looking for this quick fix, and it's really more about a paradigm shift in terms of your belief systems. RJ has to be done with the racial justice lens because the definition is it's the antidote to hundreds of years of oppression and racism in our country and to punitive ways of doing things that have disproportionately affected people of color. To do RJ without knowing that or thinking about it is to really do a disservice to it, perhaps even to support those systems. Because if you are restoring a community that is that way, then you're just perpetuating it. That's why our main priority is to create the community that we want to restore to. And that's really hard to do in a system and an institution that really wants it to be a certain way because it's been 150 years of these mechanisms that have been put in place during slavery and the Middle Passage. So to try and be the antidote to that takes consciousness and intentionality.

When we first started doing RJ, we always had an eye for doing this. We thought at first, yes, we're doing this to end the school to prison pipeline and to end our racial disparities. And just simply by doing that we will accomplish that eventually. I think at some point along the line we realized, no, actually, RJ is not going to do that just by doing RJ. You have to be much more intentional about it and really think about, where are the lever points for that work? And from what I've been able to determine, it's the adults that really need to understand, to look in the mirror and understand our own biases and hooks and triggers and how they play out and what that does.

So we're very intentional about talking about that and pursuing that track in our RJ work. Our district has a whole office of equity. We have someone who coordinates antiracist education and curriculum. We have a very progressive mindset when it comes to that. So we work closely with those other people in our district doing that work, and we support training and coaching of teachers to understand that.

I don't think we're doing enough. We always have to rethink how we're doing it and what's working, what's not working. We've dropped our suspensions by more than half, but they're still disproportionate. It's still Black kids that are suffering more than anyone else in our district. I don't think we've been successful yet, and I think it's going to be a lot. It takes more than restorative justice.

But that doesn't mean we don't try. There's this concept of race from Michael White and relayed to me by David Anderson Hooker: When you're talking about race in a conversation, it's usually absent but always implicit. We try to keep that in mind and talk about it. When there is conflict, usually among adults, we usually bring up race during the prep—is that a factor in this? Where does race play out here? Not just race, but power and privilege. We try to have that conversation with people prior to everybody meeting so that we understand what's often unsaid but is so influential on whatever the situation is. We don't shy away from it. I've done work with other school districts. I will go around the country and do trainings, and a lot of places I've gone, they're like, Oh no, we don't talk about that.

What are your thoughts on where the movement is in general? Do you feel like it's being co-opted in some ways?

You have to be very careful not to co-opt the work. I think that's something we've tried very hard not to do really intentionally. I hope we're not. I'm sure we probably are in some way. But we're trying really hard to honor the Indigenous ancestral origins of this work, and I do have the occasion to speak to people around the country that are implementing this, and it is doomed to fail at most of those places; I can tell just by the way they're talking about it and by the level of commitment they want to give to it. They want to plug and play. They don't necessarily want to talk about race. They don't want to commit to something as heavy a lift as RJ. They want to just come in and fix really broken, harmful systems within a year, and they only want to see it as a practice for dealing with harm and not as a way to build and maintain community. They're going to end up giving RJ a bad name.

I never try to convince people. If they want to know, I'll tell them how to do it and then show them, and I'll help them do it. But even in OUSD, people all the time say to me, especially people who take our trainings, like, "This should be mandated for everybody." And I'm like, "You can't make people do it." It's one of our foundational principles. It has to be voluntary. It'll make you go crazy if you worry too much about the people who aren't doing it or the people who don't get it. You can't be the gatekeeper for all that. You just have to let it go and influence who you can, and work with the people that are like, "Yes, please."

Is there anything that you want to put out there in the universe that we haven't touched on yet?

For people who are already implementing some kind of SEL curriculum—RJ does not replace anything good that you're doing. If you're doing something good, then RJ can just support it. It can be there as a way to be more inclusive and equitable, a space for dialogue. If you've got a really good community in your classroom or in your school and it's solid—people feel connected; you walk in, parents walk in, they feel welcome; students are connected to each other; staff are connected to each other; relationships are present; and people are operating from them—then RJ doesn't necessarily need to be the thing that does that. Most schools *don't* have that going on, and so RJ does come in and do that first.

But RJ can then just be used as a method for dialogue, for talking about things, and then, of course, yes, responding to harm and conflict and providing individual support for students or staff who need it individually. But you don't need to replace anything good. If it's good, keep it. RJ can help you do that in a way, so that's one thing I think is important.

Also, I think it's important that people understand that trauma is real. RJ needs to be done not only with a racial justice lens but also with a lens that's healing-centered, that is trauma-informed. Understanding behavior through that lens, understanding communities through that lens and the work in general, that's something that's really important.

And that this is a long-term thing. This isn't something that's gonna happen in one to three years. It takes deep commitment from the top. If you're at a school and the principal's like, "Sure, go ahead! Do RJ!" That's not [shakes head]. The principal has to understand what it is, want to do it, support it, expect it, and check in on it. It doesn't mean they are the ones who have to do it all the time, but it does mean that it needs to come from that level, and they need to message that out. So schools need to slow down, strategize, and think, Is this something we really want to spend time on? Because it's going to be a big commitment. And if the answer is yes, then they can really do it. It's not just something that you're going to have someone come in and do. Magic happens during it, but it's not a magic wand.

36

Learning From Implementation Science

With any new initiative—including restorative practices—the school community should first establish a need and then gather information. While this can sometimes be a more organic process, as was the case with OUSD's restorative justice program, it is important to consider a long-term vision and a firm goal. This ensures that initiatives are not only rolled out with fidelity but also able to have longevity. Nothing is worse than one more education fad that fizzles out until the next new thing comes along. Any teacher or school leader can tell you that initiative fatigue is real.

We can take a few cues from the field of implementation science, which is the "methods or techniques used to enhance the adoption, implementation, and sustainability" of a program or practice (Eccles & Mittman, 2006). While there are varying frameworks for the stages of implementing a program, the National Implementation Research Network (2020) identifies the following (see Figure E-1):

1. **Exploration:** This is the identification stage, where needs, fit, and feasibility are assessed.

2. **Installation:** In this planning stage, resources and supports are identified and developed.
3. **Initial implementation:** During this period of getting started, practices are initiated and data is collected to improve supports.
4. **Full implementation:** This stage centers on improvement, consistency, and measuring outcomes.

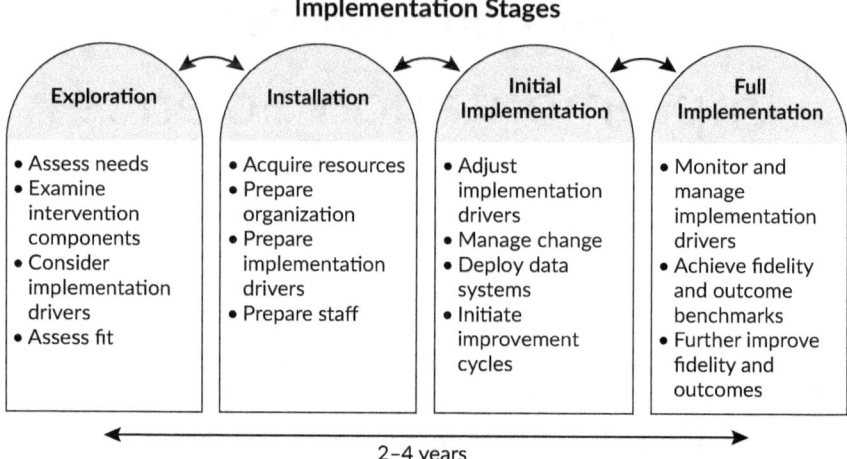

FIGURE E-1: Implementation stages in implementation science (adapted from the SISEP Center, University of North Carolina at Chapel Hill, 2012)

Table E-1 includes an example of a first-year plan for getting started with restorative practices at your school. In the next chapter, we will explore how Edgar utilized a similar plan when he first wrestled with whole-school implementation.

It is important to note that the various stages of implementation do not necessarily follow in a linear fashion, and many of the steps involved in one stage may be happening simultaneously with steps from another stage. In addition, as you consider potential implementation plans, remember that sustainability should trump scale. Start this work in smaller chunks rather than biting off more than you can chew. As you craft your implementation plan, make sure you also attach a timeline to each step. And as we reach the later stages of implementation, we need to simultaneously consider processes for improvement.

TABLE E-1: Sample Whole-School RP Implementation Plan—Year 1

STAGE	QUESTIONS TO CONSIDER
1: Exploration	• What is the vision for what RP might look like at your particular school? • Who can serve on your school's RP team (e.g., principal, school counselor, teacher leader)? • What school climate and discipline data can be gathered to assess why this work is necessary? • What are the preferred outcomes of whole-school RP implementation? How will these outcomes be measured? • What trainings are available for the RP team?
2: Installation	• How will the school's RP vision be introduced to the staff? • What are ways that the whole staff can be trained in tier 1 practices? • What are systems of support that are provided for the RP team and the whole staff? What will ongoing PD, dialogue, and problem-solving look like? • What tools will be used to monitor progress and fidelity? • How will students and families be informed of and involved in these processes?
3: Initial implementation	• Where and how will tier 1 strategies be implemented? What are existing structures in which these strategies can be infused? What are new lever points that can be created? • What will consistent community building and celebrations look like, and how can those be built into the school day/year? • What will ongoing progress monitoring look like?
4: Full implementation	• What are the measured outcomes so far? • What are ways that school policies can be adjusted to align with the RP plan? • What are areas of improvement? How will improvements result in sustainability and fidelity of the program? • If feasible, what are areas that can be scaled up? What will supports and training look like?

37

A Time for Change: Edgar's Story

We began this text by telling you about how the three of us—Mirko, Pam, and Edgar—were connected through our own walks with restorative practices. Using his proven experience with restorative practices at Boston Arts Academy, Edgar helped plant the seed at Mirko and Pam's school community at the Putnam Avenue Upper School, and the three of us witnessed transformations in each of our school communities when we centered relationships and healing. We wrap up our time with you by going back to the beginning and sharing with you how Edgar successfully launched school-wide restorative practices at Boston Arts Academy. This was not because he leaned into any set curriculum per se, but because he focused on restorative practices as a way of being and believing. Part of those beliefs involve understanding the importance of centering community, healing, and racial and social justice.

We open with Edgar describing his initiation, so to speak, into his new work environment as a first-year administrator, one in which the adults were right and the students were wrong. Next, Edgar will continue to describe his school's journey as they moved from the stage of exploration and fact-finding to installation and implementation. As you learn about Edgar's experience, we advise you to read it by putting on a UDL lens.

Edgar's firm goal was incorporating restorative practices as a way of life at the school and following general phases of implementation, but there is also room for variability in what he did to make those phases possible based on the needs of the learners—adults and students alike—in front of him.

I was brought in for change. I want to believe that I was recruited as an administrator at the Boston Arts Academy, one of the city's only public high schools for the visual and performing arts, because I was highly recommended for my years of experience and for my skill sets in cultivating and fostering a positive school climate and culture, being an advocate and a champion for students, and helping them develop their voices. In my first year as a high school administrator, I was enthusiastic and excited to have gotten the position, but I was also humbled by it. I recall also being overwhelmed with anxiety and preoccupied with the feeling that I was not going to be able to transfer and apply what I knew when it came to students.

During my interview, I was told that I would oversee the ninth- and tenth-grade student body and that I would be the point person to manage discipline for those grade levels. At the time, the student body was a little over 350 students. On my first day at the high school, I was immersed in their incoming student summer orientation week. I was going to meet the incoming ninth-grade class while I, too, was new to the school; we would be going on the same journey as "freshmen."

On the first day of summer orientation, the co-headmaster requested to meet. She informed me that a group of upperclassmen were scheduled to be at the school with their parents regarding an incident that took place over the summer during a school-sponsored trip. I was taken aback and confused because I recalled during my interview that I would be engaging only with the ninth and tenth graders in terms of discipline. Entering the room, I observed that the students and parents were sitting in chairs arranged in a U-shape. I was seated at a long table directly in front of them with the co-headmasters, a student support member, and the teacher who accompanied the students on this trip. As I sat there, I realized that I was being initiated into the school by sitting in on a group disciplinary hearing for the students and their parents.

As the hearing was being conducted, I immediately began to recognize that the students were not being heard and were not being allowed to express themselves freely to share their experience and their truth of the events. The disciplinary hearing was conducted in such a way that the adults were right and the students were wrong. The students were not given due process, and the only outcome and solution provided was generated by the adults in the room. This first experience at the high school gave me a glimpse of what I was about to walk into.

YEAR 1: EXPLORATION

In my first year as a dean of students, I wanted to learn all about the current climate and culture of the school to determine what I was going to be taking on. I wanted to assess the needs of the student body and gather information that would help me better understand how staff interacted with students and what, if any, their expectations of students were. In my initial months, I was able to quickly gather that many students had a profound relationship with their assigned advisors of four years. The advisor was the student's go-to person at the school when issues came up, so if anyone knew a student well, it was the advisor. I also noted that many students sought the nurturing care provided by members of the student support team. They also sought out the school nurse, and many others gravitated to one of the co-headmasters. I got the sense that students knew they had an adult at the school that they could approach when needed.

Many of the staff were veterans in the education world and already had established norms and expectations within their pedagogy and classroom management. It was obvious that most of the staff catered to the needs of their advisees and not of their students. This observation led me to believe that favoritism was how certain advisees got opportunities and exceptions, such as having their absences from school excused for circumstances beyond their control, because their advisor would strongly advocate for them and intervene. But when a student didn't have an influential advisor and attempted to advocate on their own behalf, their voice was not taken into consideration.

I shifted my focus and began to pay attention to how the classroom environments were being managed and how the lessons of the class centered student voice. In some classes, the learning approach was very traditional—teacher in front of the class and students behind desks—but in others, students engaged in group work and activities, or used some form of circles to engage with each other and with the lesson. I noticed that not everyone was having the same learning experience or being provided a space to engage and actively participate in their learning; they were simply expected to absorb the instruction. There was inconsistency throughout the school. This was difficult for students to grasp and process, as this inconsistency was also reflected in how students were graded, how students and staff communicated, and where they could go for answers.

My next task was to examine current interventions (i.e., the school discipline policy) to learn how they were being managed and whether they were effective. My crash course was the disciplinary hearing mentioned earlier, which was conducted with a very punitive approach and with no consideration for the student's voice or the process. Essentially, those students were told what to do to fix the problem. They were not given a space to process the wrongdoing, take accountability, understand their choices and their impact on themselves and others, and take responsibility and do right by those they did wrong. There were many incidents of student conflict that resulted in out-of-school exclusion, no space for reconciliation, and no offer of mediation. The many incidents of negative dynamics between students and staff led to an unhealthy relationship, resulting in the student being wronged and the staff having the upper hand. The students were left with the understanding that when it came to poor choices they had made or breaches of school rules, they were not going to be heard and would be punished.

Despite this, the students came to school eager to belong to something and to be provided with safety and consistency. My job was to ensure that they were going to be heard and understood, to provide a safe school life, and to teach them how to take responsibility and to do right when they did wrong. The ultimate goal was to instill in them the desire to not do wrong to others just as they did not want wrong done to them.

YEAR 2: INSTALLATION AND INITIAL IMPLEMENTATION

In my second year, I created a goal to reduce out-of-school suspension by half. This goal was going to require a culture shift and would make some teaching staff uncomfortable when addressing discipline. An important resource during this installation phase was one of my colleagues. I began by developing trust with this colleague, who believed in my work and was offering full support. Then, to my administrative team, I proposed that I pilot both mediation and restorative practices for some students who often found themselves violating school rules, and I was given the green light to do so. My team gave me their backing for this endeavor and their full trust in my expertise and execution.

I developed and created a small pilot program for students who had violated school rules. Just as students made choices that led to their facing consequences in school, I wanted them to have another set of choices for restoring harm and doing right. In the initial phase of the pilot, when a student was in violation, I would sit with them and we would thoroughly discuss why they made the choice. We would go through the list of people who may have been harmed and how their choice might have impacted the culture of the school and any other community they belonged to. After this initial process, I would give them the option to recognize and restore the harm they'd caused, sharing with me what that would look like and feel like, or to go through the traditional process of sitting in a formal disciplinary hearing with their guardian.

Most students that year opted to restore the harm simply because they thought it was an easy way out and it wouldn't require their parents to sit in an office with us. I believe that in fact this was not the easiest way out, because it required them to really look at themselves and learn what had led them to their choices and to develop empathy for those they'd harmed. It required them to look at the ways in which their actions had a trickle effect. They would then have to think about how and what they could possibly do to repair what they'd done to others.

Restoring harm took various forms depending on the specific harm done and its severity. Students were willing to sit in on mediations and save face in the presence of the other party, repair physical damages they caused, and stand in front of their community and express genuine remorse for their actions. The students that chose to repair harm and sit in on mediations had the most astounding impact on those they had directly harmed and on the community. They demonstrated a significant decrease in poor choices and negative behaviors; began to intervene in situations involving other students that previously would have required adults to get involved; and developed de-escalation skills to defuse incidents of conflict and tension. They began to refer students to me so that I could help them resolve the problem and "not get in trouble" or have their parents come in. I laughed when I realized that students were perceiving my new way of handling discipline with them as the easy way out when, in reality, it required more work, time, and energy from all parties. However, it built a true sense of restoring harm, trust, safety, and a healthy way of coexisting in the school environment.

The students who opted to face a formal disciplinary hearing found themselves being excluded from the school and falling behind in school work. The students who opted to restore harm and/or sit in mediations were on an upward trend in school progress and performance, something staff and advisors took notice of. They were impressed with the outcome and by the students' greater sense of maturity, responsibility, and commitment to school life. Other staff grew more wary and expressed concerns that opting out of traditional disciplinary measures might have a negative impact, such as possible recurrences of misbehavior and distrust among adults and students, on the greater school community. They preferred that *all* students in violation of the rules be taught a lesson by being excluded from the school so that the school community wouldn't be disrupted and so they wouldn't have to deal with the "troublemakers." These reactions, particularly from the adults who had little to no skills in classroom and individual student management, were expected and anticipated. These were teachers who continuously excluded students from their classrooms for very minimal defiant behaviors and for classroom insubordination.

As part of our improvement cycle, we examined our suspension data. Although I was not able to cut my numbers by half, by the end of the school year, I had significantly decreased out-of-school suspension, and I was content with that outcome. I also had won the trust of the majority of the students when it came to student and adult relationships, but most importantly they trusted that I had their best interests at heart and would listen to them to achieve the best possible outcome when they were faced with disciplinary consequences.

In anticipation of our full implementation phase for the next school year, the administrative team reconvened during the summer to consider a formal overhaul of school policies and procedures as it related to school discipline. But it was also important to highlight the need for the teaching staff to be on board with the new initiative. As we went into our staff summer professional development, we decided that we would have a very different experience than what everyone was accustomed to. We planned a week-long RP experience, knowing that in order for staff to truly understand the impact of restorative practices within a school community, they were going to be immersed in RP's philosophy and beliefs. They were going to experience and feel how restorative practices impact individuals and benefit the greater community.

YEAR 3 AND ON: FULL IMPLEMENTATION

As I entered my third year at the high school, the goal was to continue to decrease any out-of-school exclusion but also to minimize academic disruption for any student in violation of school rules, unless their behavior was egregious enough that it threatened the safety of a member of the school community and made teaching and learning impossible. To continue to work on staff buy-in, I strengthened my relationships with key staff members, coached and mentored staff on classroom management and student management, and identified where and how restorative practices were part of the school already. During my first two years at the school, I'd observed that some teachers used some variation of restorative practices—such as concentric circles, fishbowl circles, and/or Socratic circles—in their classrooms as a way to deliver instructional lessons to their students. This was important for me to acknowledge to the teaching staff because they needed to know that they weren't starting from ground zero with restorative practices, that indeed they already were experts in some variation of it, and that there was an existing foundation in place at the school.

To help the staff get on board with the new rollout with restorative practices, the administration team wanted to recruit teacher champions—those who believed and used restorative practices naturally and intentionally with their students. This strategy was intended to make believers out of the remaining few holdouts. The goal was to intentionally use restorative practices in all aspects of the school, from staff meetings to classroom-based lessons, and most importantly to make sure they were student-centered. The administrative staff began implementing the practices during our school-wide staff meetings to model as well as to demonstrate their commitment to and belief in them.

This culture shift rocked the school's foundational pedagogical belief. We knew that we needed to scaffold the learning curve for the staff. We began by making it an expectation that they would use restorative practices to engage and interact with their advisees when they met with them twice a week. We would provide them with exemplar prompts to engage in discussion or, if they were comfortable, they could create and use their own prompts. These set of expectations began to be ingrained as a way of school life, and it was apparent that the use of restorative practices was making a positive impact on students. We checked in with the students and learned that the majority of them felt they were being heard, acknowledged, and recognized during the process. The implementation of restorative practices in the school fostered a sense of belonging to the school community that recognized student voice and presence.

We also decided to get content team teachers to make restorative practices live in the curriculum. This was not as successful as we wanted it to be, but a few content teachers got on board. Having had a summer of planning and a week-long professional development, a set of teachers were determined to ensure that their students were at the center of teaching and learning. These teachers utilized restorative practices in the daily lessons of their curriculum. As they began to use the practices appropriately and with integrity, they transformed their classroom culture. There was a significant decrease in negative incidents in those classrooms and much more student engagement and participation. This success happened in parallel with using the practices during advisory and staff meetings, getting students trained, and addressing harm at the school with the practices.

It was clear that our students were on board as well. With many of my students having experienced restorative practices for mostly disciplinary reasons and having a significant decrease in results with out-of-school suspension, it was evident that these practices and beliefs, which I held to be fundamentally true, were working. Students genuinely trusted me with the process of handling discipline and utilizing restorative practices as a means to address the negative impact. Students were developing, acquiring, and utilizing social-emotional skills through the RP process and began to think of themselves and others as highly valued members of the school community.

To make my work more efficient, I needed to build capacity, so I entrusted one of my colleagues who oversaw student activities. We knew we needed to get students involved in the process and that to maintain their buy-in, we needed them to trust not only me but also each other and to believe that this was a much better approach to wrongdoing for all members of the community. My colleague and I identified a small group of students with social clout in the student body for training as restorative practice keepers who would help facilitate conversations and restorative justice circles to restore harm done to others.

Every year from then on, we trained a group of 15–20 students to ensure that we had enough students we could call on to facilitate the practices. These students were in Grades 9–12 and from different academic backgrounds; I was targeting high academic achievers as well as students who may have struggled with their grades but had social capital within the school community. These particular students had innate social skills, and, when called upon to facilitate restorative practices in front of others, they began to transform into student leaders, advocating for themselves and others while maintaining their true sense of self. Their growth and maturity became obvious to school staff. I was also very proud of the students who volunteered, as the RP process forced them out of their shells; they began to self-identify as students in the school who had a voice and could advocate for themselves and others.

Starting that year, restorative practices were introduced to the incoming class every summer during orientation week. They would be immersed in different activities to get an authentic experience that would surface different feelings, preparing them for what restorative practices would be like at the school. Some students knew of restorative practices but had not experienced them, while others had never heard of them. It was critical that incoming students understand why and how the school used restorative practices.

As we monitored the progress and outcomes of our school-wide RP launch, we were getting a surge of requests from both students and teachers, in parent/teacher meetings and school-wide conversations, to use restorative practices. Teachers began to request restorative practices when they needed to have difficult conversations with parents. They requested facilitation support and a menu of prompts to keep the conversation focused on supporting the student's needs versus on the student themselves. Typically, these meetings would assign the student full ownership of their educational success or demise. But implementing some RP prompts and ways of facilitating the conversation changed the focus and distributed ownership among the teacher, parent, and the student, making the conversation about the student's successes or challenges more beneficial and productive.

When supporting a request to facilitate school-wide conversations, we realized we needed to be mindful of the topics to be discussed. Some required more in-depth preparation and needed someone especially skilled to facilitate a restorative practice circle. These shifts came during a time when the nation was facing uproar with police brutality and violence toward Black and Brown people. At the school level, student leaders wanted to have a space to share what they were being exposed to, whether in the news, social media, or in their personal conversations with others. This prompted them to ask for restorative circles during school hours, and they wanted all members of the school community to have the opportunity to be part of a conversation. This change allowed all members of the school community to have a space to be acknowledged and recognized, their voices present and on a platform to be heard.

As more and more students experienced and were immersed in the practices, there were more and more requests to address negative classroom dynamics and conflict among students and with staff. These requests allowed us to build our resources of students who were trained to help defuse and resolve conflict among their peers. The school was able to scale up our practices and create another initiative—revamping the school discipline policy and deploying a student-led and focused way of addressing discipline. It was then that the peer restorative practice review was born.

When students were facing a disciplinary hearing for violating the code of conduct, they were given another option: to be part of a peer review to establish harm and to restore any harm caused. This option was presented in cases when peer review was appropriate and necessary. Students who led these reviews came from all grade levels. These reviews were always led by two students; most of the time, I was not present, which allowed the process to unfold in an organic and genuine way among the students.

As for the guardians, parents, and families, we were receiving positive feedback on our school culture and community through direct communications and through surveys sent by the superintendent's office. Guardians spoke of how animated and excited their child was about school and how they felt like they made the right choice by coming, a result due in large part to our restorative practices and beliefs. Students often shared that they found themselves facilitating familial conflicts using the principles and practices of restorative justice. This was rewarding to hear—these types of promising testimonials solidified our belief in advocating for and holding restorative practices as a way of life.

38

Pause and Reflect On Part E

SUMMARY

To succeed with restorative practices, we need to be both proactive and reflective. As outlined in previous chapters of this text, restorative practices are not a reactive response to conflict, but rather a proactive structure that facilitates voice, and we get the most out of it by using it flexibly for different contexts. The old adage "practice makes progress" certainly applies here. Once we normalize the use of voice so that it is apparent in all aspects of school life, its power to resolve conflict grows exponentially. By normalizing vulnerability, centering our work on providing young people with agency, and instituting structures that support it—and by lifting up our learners' voices, experiences, and perspectives—we can heal our schools, systems, and the culture within them.

REFLECTION QUESTIONS

1. How does the concept that the various stages of implementation are not always linear, and steps in one stage may overlap with those in another stage, resonate with your journey in implementing restorative practices in your school?

2. How can the principle of prioritizing sustainability over scale, as mentioned in the text, inform your approach to introducing restorative practices within your educational setting?

3. In what ways did your experiences align with the idea that restorative practices are not cookie-cutter strategies and that context and prerequisites like trust, openness to feedback, and commitment to equity are crucial for success?

4. How did the demonstration of restorative circles during the staff introduction session align with the idea of using experience as a means to introduce and unpack restorative practices?

5. What strategies and approaches can you derive from Edgar's journey to facilitate staff engagement, and his willingness to pilot restorative practices, within your school?

PART F

Universal Design for Learning and Restorative Practices

The brain seeks to minimize social threats and maximize opportunities to connect with others in community.
—Zaretta Hammond, author of
Culturally Responsive Teaching and the Brain

39

What Is Universal Design for Learning?

I DON'T HAVE TIME FOR ONE MORE NEW THING

PAM CHU-SHERIFF

I still remember the bright and sunny afternoon over half a decade ago when Mirko walked into my office and handed me a book. At the time, Mirko and I were the principal and assistant principal, respectively, of the Putnam Avenue Upper School in Cambridge. "I have something for you to read," he said with a knowing smile. Already annoyed, I hardly looked up from my computer screen. After years of working together, Mirko and I are like family, but we also have had our days when he would play the annoying older brother, and I was the bratty little sister. I was in true form that afternoon.

Continuing to type, I replied, "I'm not reading it. I don't have time for one more new thing." I glanced over at the copy of *Katie Novak's UDL Now!: A Teacher's Guide to Applying Universal Design for Learning in Today's Classrooms* that he had placed on my desk. Just to be extra, I added, "And I don't like the cover." Not wanting to poke the bear, Mirko quickly retreated to his office. Little did I know that I would later eat my words, and in a big way.

I now work as a consultant, proselytizing to audiences across the country and beyond about the wonders of not only restorative practices but also UDL after having witnessed both transform the lives of our staff and students.

We've established that restorative practices represent both a framework and range of approaches that aim to develop community and relationships and to prevent and repair conflict and harm. Like restorative practices, UDL is a student-centered framework, and we will illustrate in this part how restorative practices align with the UDL's fundamental tenet of providing students with voice and agency. When restorative practices are viewed through a UDL lens, we can expand our conceptual frameworks and add to our educator toolkits to ensure that all students are included, valued, supported, and empowered.

So what exactly is Universal Design for Learning? It's an educational framework grounded in decades of research in both neuroscience and learning that allows educators to proactively plan for barriers in their lesson design, give students voice and choice in their learning, and challenge and support all students, regardless of their differences.

The core beliefs of a UDL practitioner, adapted from Novak and Couros (2022), are:

1. Variability is the rule, not the exception.

2. All students can work toward the same firm goals and grade-level standards with flexible means and adequate support.

3. All learners can develop agency, creativity, and innovation when barriers are removed.

Let's take a look at the first core belief: **learner variability**. It might sound like common sense to say that every child is different. However, as educators, are we merely paying lip service to our students' differences while secretly thinking, *Why can't you all be like Student X? That would* *make my life so much easier.* We've definitely been there. Or in true UDL fashion, do we expect, accept, and celebrate that there is no such thing as an average learner, and as a result, not try to shape our students into that mythical mold? Again, it may be easy to theoretically accept that students all bring a unique mix of strengths and weaknesses and everything in between, yet how often do we still teach every student in the same way at the same time?

The next core belief centers on the notion that we must start with **firm goals** and grade-level standards. There is flexibility with how to achieve those goals, but the goals themselves are fixed. Lowering expectations because, say, we feel sorry for our students is actually doing them a disservice. While well intentioned, we are actually reinforcing inequities if all of our students don't have access to grade-level standards. The key, though, is that we have flexibility in the supports and scaffolds we provide students with in order to reach those sometimes lofty goals. One of Pam's hesitations about UDL on that fateful day when Mirko brought that book into her office was the concern that, with its emphasis on voice and choice, UDL was some New Age–speak for letting kids run amok and do whatever they wanted while the cold reality of standards, standardized testing, and the real world was only going to further marginalize already marginalized students. After Pam finally decided to crack open that book and started learning more about UDL, she realized that UDL does in fact align with high-expectations teaching.

The last core belief focuses on **learner agency and removing barriers**. While we are well on our way in this 21st century, it seems impossible to keep up with all of the latest technological advances, and the pace at which our young people are learning some of the latest trends is astounding. *The Future of Jobs Report 2020* from the Platform for the New Economy and Society at the World Economic Forum found that the top 10 skills of 2025 were analytical thinking and innovation; active learning and learning strategies; complex problem-solving; critical thinking and analysis; creativity, originality, and initiative; leadership and social influence; technology use, monitoring, and control; technology design and programming; resilience, stress tolerance, and flexibility; reasoning, problem-solving, and ideation. Many of us might not have been exposed to any of these skills when we were students, but times are changing, especially in education, whether we like it or not. Novak and Couros (2022) describe many of these skills as next-generation skills and group them into four key domains: core subjects and skills, learning and innovation skills, career and life skills, and productivity and accountability (see Table F-1).

TABLE F-1: Key Domains for Next-Generation Skills (Source: Novak & Couros, 2022)

KEY DOMAINS	ESSENTIAL NEXT-GENERATION SKILLS
Core subjects and skills	• Reading • Writing • Numeracy
Learning and innovation skills	• Critical thinking • Problem-solving • Communications • Creativity and innovation
Career and life skills	• Collaboration and teamwork • Leadership and responsibility • Initiative and self-direction • Flexibility and adaptability • Social and cross-cultural interaction • Career and self-reliance
Productivity and accountability	• Digital literacy skills • Computing literacy • Information literacy • Media literacy

In light of these next-generation skills, the goal of UDL is not to produce straight-A students. As CAST (2024) puts it, the goal of UDL is learner agency that is purposeful and reflective, resourceful and authentic, and strategic and action-oriented.

When it comes to removing barriers, unfortunately, there are so many different barriers to learning that we can categorize them into different spheres. But before you start feeling overwhelmed or discouraged, be assured that the flip side of identifying barriers means that we can also discuss ways to overcome them. And that anticipation of barriers and proactive planning is what UDL is all about—it's all in the design. UDL focuses on removing barriers to learning through three principles (CAST, 2024), shown in Figure F-1:

1. **Multiple means of engagement:** The "why" of learning
2. **Multiple means of representation:** The "what" of learning
3. **Multiple means of action and expression:** The "how" of learning

The Universal Design for Learning Guidelines

The goal of UDL is **learner agency** that is purposeful & reflective, resourceful & authentic, strategic & action-oriented.

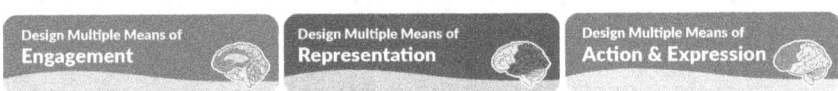

FIGURE F-1: The Universal Design for Learning principles

Let's consider the engagement principle. Although sometimes met with annoyance or offense, that age-old student question—"Why are we learning this?"—should really be one of the central questions in our planning. The engagement principle is all about the why. What really motivates our students to learn? As educators, we may consciously or subconsciously consider compliance—*Are students doing what I'm telling them to do?*—as the gold standard in our classroom environment. Especially if we are struggling with classroom management, our main objective might be just making sure that students aren't chasing each other around the room with scissors. Who has time to think about whether students care what they're learning about?

It goes without saying that having a sense of order in the classroom is significant not only for students' physical safety but also for their social and emotional well-being. But we need to push beyond simply teaching our students to be rule followers. At the Putnam Avenue Upper School, Mirko and Pam used to conduct classroom walkthroughs where one of our "look-fors" was tracking data on engagement based on Schlechty's (2011) five levels of student engagement (see Figure F-2).

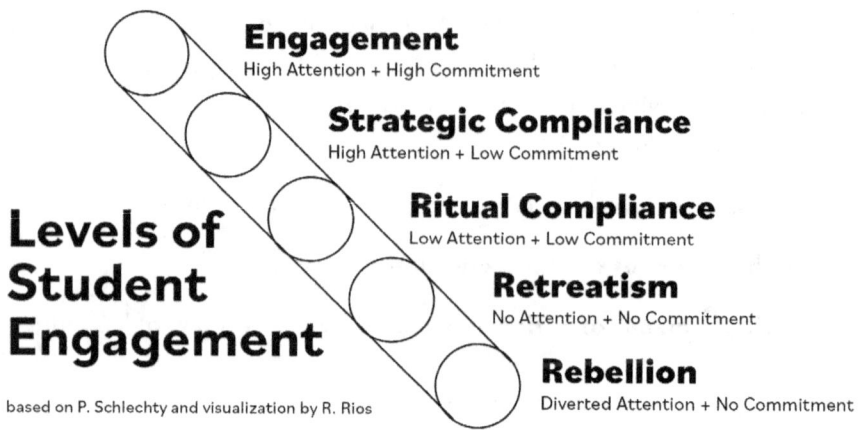

FIGURE F-2: Schlechty's levels of student engagement (source: Novak Education)

According to this framework, the lowest level of engagement is *rebellion*, in which students refuse to do the assigned task, are disruptive, or try to replace the assigned task with their own activities. This is, say, kids chasing each other around the room with scissors. Next is *retreatism*, which is characterized by students who aren't engaged in the work and aren't compliant, but are not being disruptive to the rest of the class. Think of the kid with the hoodie on and earbuds in or the student with their head down on the desk. Higher up on the scale is *ritual compliance*, in which the work has little or no immediate meaning to students, but there are extrinsic, valuable outcomes that keep them on task. There is also *strategic compliance* that describes students who work their tails off to get good grades not because they're actually invested in the class but because they want to, say, get into a good college. Finally, the highest level is *authentic engagement*, which means that students are "immersed in work that has clear meaning and immediate value to them" (Schlechty, 2011).

After conducting each of our walkthroughs, we would compile the percentage of classrooms that were at each level of student engagement and then share the results with staff (for example, "30% of classrooms had authentic engagement; 70% of classrooms had both ritual and strategic compliance combined"). We then set goals for the percentage of classrooms we wanted to see at each level of engagement (for instance, "We will maintain 0% rebellion and strive for 0% retreatism, 0% ritual compliance, 40% strategic compliance, and 60% authentic engagement"). Due to our emphasis on making learning authentically relevant, and thanks to the tireless work of our teachers, we were able to reach those goals.

Piquing student interest is so crucial when it comes to students' ability to learn. But it's important to note that engagement is more than just a one-off parlor trick that captures students' attention for one fleeting moment. The engagement principle goes deeper in that it also provides options for how to sustain that attention and effort by encouraging students to develop ways that they can self-reflect so that they can also self-regulate.

The second UDL principle, representation, is all about the "what" of learning and presenting information and content in different ways. We need to recognize that students don't all perceive and comprehend information in the same way, and we need to plan accordingly. As a small but simple example, when Pam used to teach Arthur Miller's *The Crucible* to her ninth graders back in what feels like the Middle Ages, she used to go to the Boston Public Library and check out cassette tapes (remember those?) of *The Crucible* being read aloud by stage actors. This auditory addition really brought the story to life and fundamentally aided students in their comprehension of the text

Lastly, the action and expression principle, or the "how" of learning, involves differentiating ways that students can express what they know. Some students may have physical mobility impairments, while others may struggle with executive function or have language barriers. Therefore, it is critical that we provide multiple ways for students to demonstrate their knowledge. A prime example is a choice board (Figure F-3), a type of graphic organizer that allows students to choose how they will learn a concept or demonstrate mastery of a concept. Before we get caught up in the fun of the various activities and run off to, say, film a podcast tutorial, it's crucial to remember that we still need to start with the standards. Does the goal of the assessment match the overall learning goals or standard? In other words, is it *construct relevant*? Other tips to remember when using choice boards are to make sure we don't overwhelm students by offering too many choices, and also make sure that we provide exemplars, especially if some of the options and mediums provided are new to students.

CHOICE BOARD

- Before choosing a medium, consider the goal. How can you best address it?
- Make sure to compare your work to the exemplars before revising/submitting your assessment.
- Complete a self-assessment using the provided rubric.
- Don't limit yourself to a single format. In many authentic settings, creators will pair text types. For example, a scientist may present a scientific poster and also give a TED-like talk about their subject.

www.novakeducation.com

FIGURE F-3: Novak Education choice board (source: Novak Education)

As we design our lessons and consider where there may be barriers to learning, we also need to consider how to optimize choice and incorporate student voice. From a UDL perspective, when we're designing our lessons, we need to include options—carefully crafted ones—that our students can choose from. When students feel a sense of ownership over their learning, they will naturally become more invested and engaged. Students should be co-creators of their own learning experiences. Sometimes as educators, we may think we know what is best for students when we may in fact be totally off base. There's nothing worse than that adult who tries too hard to be "down" with students but is embarrassingly out of touch. So what's the easiest way to find out what students are thinking? Just ask them.

40

The Connection Between UDL and Restorative Practices

One of our go-to prompts to use with both students and adults is, "What's one word or phrase that comes to mind to describe your..." and then you can fill in that sentence stem by asking about say, everyone's week, their weekend, their school year so far, how they're feeling as a teacher, how they're feeling as a parent or caregiver, and so on. If this was asked while running a circle with students, of course, everyone would take turns passing around the talking piece and sharing their answers. We'll also use a question like this if we're running a workshop, whether it be in person or virtually with participants on the other side of the country, and people will share their answers in the chat box.

What's so effective about this quick check-in is that we are able to get a sense of where people's headspace is before we dive into a full-blown circle or professional development session. If a student or a teacher says something like "stressful," "exhausting," "super fun," or "Celtics game," we might note to follow up with that individual afterward to see how they're doing or ask about what was so fun about their weekend and build a connection from there. If we can gain insight from someone else just by asking them to share one word about their life, how much more can we learn when we engage in deeper, intentional conversations with our students?

If we examine the range of approaches within the restorative practices continuum, any one of those practices ultimately involves hearing from a student. In fact, restorative practices cannot be implemented with fidelity or success if students' voices are not authentically at the forefront. Even if we ask a student an affective question, such as, "How do you think that made Student X feel when you called her that name?" we should truly want to hear their perspective, and that can help inform what steps we take from there. If we find ourselves suddenly holding an impromptu conference with two students after an almost-scuffle at recess, we need to hear what those students have to say about it, and then we can work on finding a solution together from there. When we've held tier 2 circles with a class of students to help with classroom management and classroom culture, students' voices are absolutely essential. In fact, we would go so far as to say that it would be impossible to build an authentic classroom community without student input and feedback.

Both UDL and restorative practices, by their very nature, have opportunities for student voice baked right in. They work hand in hand, as offering "voice and choice" is central to UDL, and restorative practices are essential mechanisms that can facilitate the process of gathering voice. In fact, oftentimes, when people first learn about UDL, the phrase "voice and choice" is included in the description (think of the "optimize choice and autonomy" consideration under the engagement principle). As discussed earlier, the ultimate goal of UDL is learner agency. Reaching this goal not only requires a healthy amount of learning how to use one's voice to advocate for one's own learning but also a hefty number of teachers providing opportunities, through restorative practices, for students to use their voices in the first place.

Let's pause for a moment and revisit Mirko and Pam's experience at the Putnam Avenue Upper School to picture what this looks like in practice. In Part A, Mirko described how valuing and capturing student voice was essential in starting to shift the school's culture to one of collaboration and community. Next, Pam will walk us through how another important cultural shift was incorporating the voices of staff. Nowhere was this more evident than in the process we followed to create the school's vision and values.

41

Vision, Values, and Voice

PAM CHU-SHERIFF

As UDL practitioners, we know that all lessons must start with the end—a firm goal or objective—in mind. Similarly, in designing our ideal school culture, we knew it was paramount not only to have a clear vision statement and core values but also to allow our faculty to have a voice in what these would look like. The Putnam Avenue Upper School was created at a time when the entire district dismantled its K–8 models and created four new middle schools in their place. At its inception, our school comprised staff from three different elementary schools, each with its own culture and values, in addition to several new hires.

Creating a new vision and new values statements for our freshly formed school community was necessary to give us permission to step aside from our previous experiences; together, we would create a conceptual framework of what this new school community would be about. This could not simply be statements that were provided *to* the school community. To ensure ownership and investment, they had to come *from* the community. Given that some were still mourning the loss of their beloved former school communities and may have even felt resentment at being placed in a new setting, we knew there needed to be room for healing.

We began to work on the vision statement at our first faculty meeting. Mirko shared with the staff an initial list of words as examples of values that particularly resonated with him to start us off: *passion, pride, ownership, balance,* and *perseverance*. We then used a variety of the Center for Leadership and Educational Equity's discussion protocols as tools to allow staff to share their thoughts and reactions in structured ways. The staff came to a consensus that they wanted to stick with this initial list. The list was also shared with families and students, who also agreed that those terms best reflected what they wanted the school to be about.

Then a new dilemma emerged. We had agreed on the five words for our core values, but we all used them differently. We applied different meanings to them, which created unintentional confusion and disagreement. The only way to resolve this was to engage in a calibration process to define what these terms would mean and look like in our school community. Alongside students and caregivers, we spent a year and a half coming to a consensus and creating specific definitions that reflected how we would use these vision and values statements to support and guide our work. The process of calibrating was not easy, but it was necessary. The words of the core values resonated with all of us, and we felt pride in knowing that we, as a community, had collectively created them. This democratic process meant hours of listening sessions and revisions, but we eventually landed on the following vision and values:

> **Vision:** *At the Putnam Avenue Upper School, we believe that all of our students can and will be successful in and out of school and beyond, no matter what their circumstances are. We believe that our students are headed towards the "Good Life." That is, we believe that our students will be college-ready and will become successful and contributing members of society with the best possible quality of life. In order to live the "Good Life," students will develop a sense of mastery of our core values of passion, pride, and ownership with balance and perseverance.*
>
> **Passion:** *It is passion that drives our community towards excellence. More specifically, our passion is for the pursuit of academic*

excellence through effort and the pursuit of social justice through recognizing the different experiences that come with race, class, gender, sexual orientation, ability, and religion. We believe it is our responsibility to use our knowledge to better the world we live in.

Pride: *We take pride in our identities and the impact we have on both individuals and larger society. We think not only about the here and now, but about the future as well, considering carefully how each choice we make will impact the future of our own lives as individuals and the future of our collective community.*

Ownership: *A great school relies on a strong sense of ownership, and we demonstrate ownership through reflection and planning. By committing to goals, developing clear plans for achieving those goals, and regularly reflecting on the progress we have made towards reaching our goals, we are accountable to ourselves and to our community.*

Balance: *We believe that being well-rounded is essential to our overall success and quality of life. In addition to academic pursuits, we seek balance through participating in activities outside of school. We celebrate our academic and extracurricular interests and know that our school culture will be balanced and healthy only if it is made up of balanced and healthy individuals.*

Perseverance: *We recognize that our relentless quest towards excellence is full of obstacles and conflict. We turn stumbling blocks into stepping stones and demonstrate perseverance by identifying challenges and striving to overcome them. We choose not to see obstacles as moments of defeat but as moments to grow and make ourselves stronger.*

The process in and of itself was both healing and restorative in that the emphasis was on how the experience would communicate to all that it was being done *with* them and not *to* them. Additionally, what we landed on at the end of the process was an authentic representation of the voices of the entire school community, and that gave us a huge boost of pride and trust in one another. Oftentimes, the vision and values of schools and organizations are nothing more than wallpaper—poster printouts that teachers are obliged to hang in their classrooms and hallways; in most cases, students and staff wouldn't even be able to tell you what the words on the posters are or what they really mean. However, at Putnam Ave., because we had created these values collectively, they were the cornerstone of our school culture and were ingrained in the day-to-day life of the school.

For instance, one of our staff members wrote a core values rap that became one of the highlights of our quarterly whole-school assemblies. Students and staff would take turns coming to the stage to rap the core values while we played the beat from Busta Rhymes's "Touch It" in the background. Some kids were so excited to get up on stage that they would run to me a few days before the assembly, breathlessly asking if they could go up to "do the core values song." In addition, a requirement for all of our eighth graders was to complete an end-of-year portfolio, which involved highlights of some of their best work in relation to each of the core values. Students had months to compile their best artifacts and to compose accompanying reflection pieces, which they then presented to a panel of administrators, teachers, family members, and various community representatives. The creation of this collective vision spurred our work forward as a staff because we had ensured that all of the voices from our community were heard.

42

Returning to the "Why" of Learning

A collective vision is a powerful conduit through which to bring people together. Restorative practices, as we know, aim to do just that—to develop community and relationships. We cannot emphasize enough the importance of building community in a learning environment. A sense of belonging and connection is so important for students' social and emotional well-being, but an often overlooked reality is that an absence of connection and emotional safety is actually a neurological barrier to learning. As stated by CAST (2018), "Information that is not attended to, that does not engage learners' cognition, is in fact inaccessible. It is inaccessible both in the moment and in the future because relevant information goes unnoticed and unprocessed." Community, collaboration, and emotional safety are not just nice-to-haves, they are must-haves.

If we return to the UDL principle of engagement, or the "why" of learning, we should think of engagement as the activator that turns on the brain. Restorative circles and conferences can serve as tools to activate students' thinking and prime them for learning. When we look at each UDL principle, there are guidelines within each principle. It is worth noting that during the summer of 2024, the most updated version, UDL

Guidelines 3.0, was released, and for the first time, restorative practices are explicitly named.

The three UDL engagement guidelines are welcoming interests and identities, sustaining effort and persistence, and emotional capacity (CAST, 2024). Within each of those guidelines are considerations that offer strategies that educators can implement in their respective learning environments. While consideration 9.4, "Cultivate empathy and restorative practices" is the clearest link between UDL and restorative practices, a case could be made for a strong connection between restorative practices and almost any of the considerations under the engagement guidelines (Table F-2). These four in particular, though, stand out:

- Optimize choice and autonomy (7.1)
- Address biases, threats, and distractions (7.4)
- Foster belonging and community (8.4)
- Promote individual and collective reflection (9.3)

Whether sharing in a formal circle or during a tier 3 restorative meeting, giving students the opportunity to share their voices absolutely builds their sense of autonomy and agency. When it comes to addressing biases and minimizing threats and distractions, it all comes down to creating a safe and supportive classroom climate, which is what is achieved when we establish appropriate values and guidelines for circles or restorative meetings. These ground rules set the stage and the tone for students to feel comfortable enough to honestly share what's on their minds. The consideration of fostering collaboration and community is part and parcel of the goal of restorative practices—building community. Lastly, self-assessment and reflection are skills that naturally develop when students are encouraged to participate in tier 1 and 2 circles and in tier 3 restorative conferences.

TABLE F-2. Crosswalk of UDL Guidelines 3.0 and Restorative Practices

UDL PRINCIPLES AND CONSIDERATIONS (CAST, 2024)		RESTORATIVE PRACTICES
Engagement	Optimize choice and autonomy (7.1) • "Offering learners choices can develop agency, pride in accomplishment, and increase connection to their learning." • "Use a collaborative approach among learners and educators to co-design learning goals, activities, and tasks."	Restorative practices center on student voice and restoring agency. Teachers serve as guides and facilitators and encourage students to become agents of their own learning, and students develop skills of self-discipline and self-motivation in the process.
	Optimize relevance, value, and authenticity (7.2) • "One of the most important ways educators recruit interest is to highlight the utility and relevance of learning and to demonstrate relevance through authentic, meaningful activities." • "It is critical to provide options that optimize what is relevant, valuable, and meaningful to the learner."	Relating learning to authentic experiences is essential for student motivation and excitement. This requires getting to know students and making them feel known, as well as validating their experiences and celebrating their backgrounds. In short, the learning and the work should feel meaningful to students.
	Nurture joy and play (7.3) • "Learning environments that spark joy and nurture opportunities for play are central to the learning process." • "Further, for historically marginalized learners, finding a sense of joy can serve as an act of resistance to oppressive systems."	Central to restorative practices is building community and relationships, and these cannot be established without joy. Tier 1 restorative circles, for instance, can simply focus on team building games and having fun.

(Continued)

TABLE F-2. Crosswalk of UDL Guidelines 3.0 and Restorative Practices (*continued*)

UDL PRINCIPLES AND CONSIDERATIONS (CAST, 2024)	RESTORATIVE PRACTICES
Address biases, threats, and distractions (7.4) • "One of the most important things an educator can do is to create an accepting and supportive space for learners, in which they feel valued, supported, agentic, and encouraged to take risks, form their own opinions, and engage in dialogue." • "While the physical safety of a learning environment is of course necessary, subtler types of threats and distractions must be attended to as well. . . . The optimal instructional environment offers options that reduce threats and negative distractions for everyone to create a safe space in which learning can occur."	In order for restorative practices to be implemented with fidelity, a truly safe space must provide a sense of both physical and emotional safety. Participants should be able to explore and discuss biases that can impact the environment, acknowledge others' experiences, and extend both forgiveness and accountability.
Foster collaboration, interdependence, and collective learning (8.3) • "Collectively generating knowledge and learning from one another's diversity of ideas, perspectives, and lived experiences is central to the learning process." • "Connected to these notions of collaboration and collective learning is the idea of interdependence — a reminder that we are all interconnected, our decisions and actions impact others, and learners can support one another."	Tier 1 community circles and tier 2 repair circles are by their very nature dependent upon collaboration and collective learning, and it is this interconnectedness that builds the foundation for all restorative practices.

TABLE F-2. Crosswalk of UDL Guidelines 3.0 and Restorative Practices (*continued*)

UDL PRINCIPLES AND CONSIDERATIONS (CAST, 2024)		RESTORATIVE PRACTICES
	Foster belonging and community (8.4) • "To support learners to sustain effort and persistence—and to thrive as learners more broadly—it is critical to design learning environments where learners feel a legitimate sense of belonging and community." • "Fostering this legitimate sense of belonging and community is especially important for learners who have been historically excluded and/or marginalized."	Restorative practices are defined largely by their focus on building relationships and community. Teachers must make a concerted effort to provide opportunities, scaffolds, and supports to foster a welcoming classroom environment so that students and teachers can build relationships with each other.
	Offer action-oriented feedback (8.5) • "Action-oriented feedback is the type of feedback that offers specific comments on ways to make progress and take action toward the learning goal."	As part of building a collective of learners, all members should have opportunities to receive and provide actionable feedback on topics ranging from academics to social-emotional matters.
	Recognize expectations, beliefs, and motivations (9.1) • "Learners can set personal goals that can be realistically reached, as well as foster positive beliefs that their goals can be met." • "Learners also need to be supported to deal with frustration and anxiety when they are in the process of meeting their goals."	As we support students in developing social-emotional skills, we need to actively communicate that we care for and believe in our students in addition to providing them with tools for self-regulation.

(Continued)

TABLE F-2. Crosswalk of UDL Guidelines 3.0 and Restorative Practices (*continued*)

UDL PRINCIPLES AND CONSIDERATIONS (CAST, 2024)		RESTORATIVE PRACTICES
	Develop awareness of self and others (9.2) • "Reminders, models, and checklists can assist learners in choosing and trying an adaptive strategy for managing and directing their emotional responses to external events (e.g., strategies for coping with anxiety-producing social settings or for reducing task-irrelevant distractors) or internal events (e.g., strategies for decreasing rumination on depressive or anxiety-producing ideation)."	According to CASEL (2024a), the five main SEL competencies are self-awareness, self-management, social awareness, relationship skills, and responsible decision-making. Restorative practices help students develop these SEL skills through discussion and relationship-building.
	Promote individual and collective reflection (9.3) • "Creating opportunities for individual and collective reflection is a key way to develop emotional capacity." • "A UDL lens reminds us of the remarkable variability of learners when it comes to metacognition. Some learners will have a heightened awareness of their progress toward goals and how to learn from mistakes along the way, while other learners can benefit from more explicit instruction and modeling."	Reflection is one of the cornerstones of restorative practices. This is true for both staff and students, so educators must be careful to model self-reflection. Being able to monitor emotions is particularly important in instances where there is conflict or challenge.

TABLE F-2. Crosswalk of UDL Guidelines 3.0 and Restorative Practices *(continued)*

UDL PRINCIPLES AND CONSIDERATIONS (CAST, 2024)		RESTORATIVE PRACTICES

	Cultivate empathy and restorative practices (9.4)
	
	• "Activities that invite listening to and considering perspectives other than one's own, building communication skills, and offering content that authentically represents a diversity of lived experiences can help expand learners' empathy for one another."
	• "Empathy is a key component to restorative practices, as learners practice identifying with the perspective of others, understand the difference between intent and impact, and seek to make the learning community whole.
	  • Use a strategy such as circle practice . . . or an emotions check-in to encourage learners to learn from one another's perspectives.
	  • Co-create and facilitate classroom agreements. Specifically ask learners to add to the agreements the things they need to feel safe in the classroom.
	  • Use a protocol such as circle practice to make communal decisions about how to restore the community after an agreement has been broken."
		Now that restorative practices are named in the UDL Guidelines 3.0, we can see an increased emphasis on the importance of developing empathy and other social-emotional skills as important in themselves, but these skill sets also result in removing barriers to academic content.

(Continued)

TABLE F-2. Crosswalk of UDL Guidelines 3.0 and Restorative Practices *(continued)*

UDL PRINCIPLES AND CONSIDERATIONS (CAST, 2024)		RESTORATIVE PRACTICES

Representation	Represent a diversity of perspectives and identities in authentic ways (1.3)
	• "It is also important for learners to be exposed to the perspectives, identities, cultures, histories, and world views of others.
	  • Challenge stereotypical or harmful portrayals of people and cultures.
	  • Facilitate listening to diverse perspectives."
		There is no hierarchy when participants are in circle with each other, and there should be opportunities for all students to bring their authentic selves to the table. In addition, there should also be space for students to discuss instances of bias and injustice.

	Cultivate understanding and respect across languages and dialects (2.3) • "Promote the opportunity to share cultures and backgrounds."	As learners deepen their relationships with each other in restorative and safe spaces, they should be encouraged to share about themselves and their identities, which should also include a sense of pride in their cultural backgrounds.
	Cultivate multiple ways of knowing and making meaning (3.3) • "Diverse cultural perspectives bring unique insights and methods of understanding the world." • "Use interactive models that guide exploration and new understandings."	Being in community with one another and being in circle with one another should naturally bring out a multitude of voices and perspectives. Circle prompts and circle guidelines can be created to also lift up the importance of valuing different perspectives.

TABLE F-2. Crosswalk of UDL Guidelines 3.0 and Restorative Practices (*continued*)

UDL PRINCIPLES AND CONSIDERATIONS (CAST, 2024)		RESTORATIVE PRACTICES
Action and Expression	Set meaningful goals (6.1) • "Setting meaningful goals that are both challenging and motivating is a critical part of the learning process."	Whether the focus is on tier 1, 2, or 3 restorative practices, there should always be a goal in mind. The goal could be communal in terms of classroom behavior or building community, or it could be individual as it relates to, say, re-entering a community after harm has been caused. Whatever the case, these goals should be explicitly named and discussed.
	Anticipate and plan for challenges (6.2) • "Once a goal is set, it is important to create time and space to plan a strategy, identify useful tools, and anticipate the challenges that may surface along the way." • "Use reflection prompts to anticipate challenges and encourage strategic planning."	As learners and adolescents, our students are bound to make mistakes; this is all part of the learning and growing process. Students can support and learn from each other as they share strategies for skills such as self-management and responsible decision-making.
	Enhance capacity for monitoring progress (6.4) • "Learning cannot happen without feedback, and that means learners need a clear understanding of the progress that is being made toward the learning goal." • "Generating multiple and varied forms of feedback throughout the learning process is essential to supporting learners' growth."	If reflection is one of the cornerstones of restorative practices, then feedback is one of the building blocks. Supporting each other in community requires helping each other to grow and improve, and feedback is necessary to do so. In addition, self-awareness skills are crucial in our journey as learners.

(Continued)

TABLE F-2. Crosswalk of UDL Guidelines 3.0 and Restorative Practices (*continued*)

UDL PRINCIPLES AND CONSIDERATIONS (CAST, 2024)		RESTORATIVE PRACTICES
	Challenge exclusionary practices (6.5) • "It is imperative to create structures to learn from learners' lived experiences in order to surface exclusionary practices—as well as to address them. • Create time for regular community sessions and individual reflection sessions. • Work as individuals and as communities to name, explore, and address exclusionary practices. • Work as individuals and as communities to develop concrete and specific actions for addressing exclusionary practices and building inclusive communities. • When an exclusionary practice is uncovered, provide opportunities for healing using community-based practices such as restorative justice."	Restorative practices are inseparable from social and racial justice. Equity and inclusion must be explicitly valued and addressed in the learning environment.

Student agency, choice, and community are all inextricably woven into the threads that make up both the engagement principle and the restorative practices framework. Perhaps less obvious are the ways in which restorative practices tie in with the principles of representation and action and expression. Restorative practices are probably best known for utilizing circle practice and conferencing. However, as discussed in Chapter 22, circles can also be used to cover academic content and are powerful pedagogical options when it comes to comprehension, executive functioning, and progress monitoring, to name a few.

Lastly, there is one crucial note on barriers. The three UDL principles of engagement, representation, and action and expression serve as lenses through which we can try to foresee barriers to learning and design our lessons accordingly. Yet when we talk about removing barriers to learning, we also need to remember that what we are really talking about is how to make learning more equitable for *all* students. To truly consider equity, we need to move beyond the classroom and also examine the larger systems that are at play. Blake (2015) suggests using the following questions to help us reflect on systemic inequality in our schools or districts:

- When decisions are being made, how is "Who has a voice and who is left out?" represented?
- How are who benefits and who suffers reflected across race, class, gender, and religious lines?
- Who determines if and why a given practice is fair or unfair, and what is their identity and background?
- What is required to create change, and who is responsible?
- What alternatives can we imagine if we reimagine our system? What would change and why?

The question of whose voices are and are not included is an essential one. When we look at our classrooms, we want to ensure that we level the playing field of our learning environments so that all students feel safe and empowered enough to even use their voices to begin with. Aside from our students, we need to consider how and how often parent and caregiver voices are given a chance to be heard. We need to be wary of the sometimes knee-jerk reaction to listen to the most vocal, well-resourced families, and we need to examine whether traditionally under-represented voices are given equal opportunities and weight, especially when it comes to families who may not have the resources or social capital to navigate an educational system that some may feel has not always had their children's best interests in mind. Lastly, when it comes to our faculty, teacher voice in the classroom is usually a given, but how often is teacher input evident in decision-making at the school or district level? As we consider how inclusive we are across students, families, or teachers, we must also reflect upon how inclusive we are within each of these groups when it comes to various demographic markers such as race, socioeconomic status, and language.

Let's take another moment to pause and consider what this looks like on the ground. In Part A, Mirko walked us through the importance of intentionally listening to student voice while he was head of the Putnam Avenue Upper School, and then earlier in this part, Pam took us through how the voices of Putnam Ave. faculty members were also incorporated at the decision-making level while creating the school's vision and core values. As we conclude this chapter by asking all of us to reflect on equity of voice, we'd like you to join us on one more trip down Putnam Ave. memory lane as we discuss the efforts we took to include family and caregiver voice.

43

Community Conversations

PAM CHU-SHERIFF

The student body at the Putnam Avenue Upper School was the most ethnically diverse in the district, with our students' families speaking over 25 different languages. We also had the highest percentage of students of color, hovering somewhere between 65% and 75%, compared to other middle schools in the city of Cambridge. About three quarters of our students were considered low-income, and about a third were on IEPs. Interestingly enough, our school building is located between two of the most prestigious universities in the world, Harvard University and the Massachusetts Institute of Technology, which are both less than a mile away from our campus. Right next door to our school building, about 200 feet away, were housing projects in which many of our students lived. As a result, we had a small number of students whose families were extremely well off and highly educated and students whose families had, say, recently immigrated from Haiti and Bangladesh and were still getting acclimated to the country and to the English language.

That said, we intentionally accounted for the wide range of perspectives and experiences that existed within our parent and caregiver population. When designing systems and structures, we took into consideration that this could and would look different with different caregivers, that families would engage for different reasons, and these differences were not only okay but also worth celebrating. If our school was to be seen as a safe space for our families, they had to see themselves, their cultures, and their identities represented in some way, shape, or form. They were the ones who should determine what was relevant to them and worth their time.

With that in mind, we strategically designed all caregiver events to include food and child care so that the absence of these would not become barriers to attending the events. Even when our events were focused on academics, we intentionally included student performances and celebrations to appeal to and draw in a wider variety of families, to access counselors, and to chat with academic teachers and advisors. We sent communications home via email, text messages, robocalls, newsletters, and hard copy as a way of taking into consideration that different caregivers would consume information differently.

To proactively design for equity of voice, our school council meetings were structured as learning opportunities for all. Barriers to authentic family engagement in these settings are often that the most well-resourced families might take up the majority of the airtime or control the direction of the content. In anticipation of clear but unspoken tensions that might emerge due to differences in race, class, and language, we mapped out our school council learning sessions for the entirety of the year and covered a broad range of topics in order to appeal to a diversity of families. Some meetings were focused on our school's framework for restorative practices or providing opportunities for caregivers to share their stories of self; other meetings were devoted to reviewing the requirements for the eighth-grade portfolios or discussing how the staff crafted learning objectives in their lesson planning.

In addition, against the backdrop of increasing racial animosity not only in the district but across the country, we also endeavored to take steps toward healing some of these tensions and toward building relationships. We decided to hold a series of events three to four times a year that we called Community Conversations: Identity and Diversity. The essential question for these events was always, "How do we promote positive identity development for our children?" The aim was to create a structure that was universally designed, one that considered what constituted community, who the community was made of, what their needs were, and what potential barriers could stand in the way. To truly be restorative, these events would have to be safe and welcoming, with multiple entry points for different types of individuals. We worked with a professor and an education consultant who crafted presentations on topics such as ethnic and racial identity and who helped facilitate discussions with a wide range of caregivers, community members from neighborhood youth centers, and even school committee representatives. Several of our staff voluntarily attended each event as well, which, considering that the events were held on a weekday evening for two and a half hours, is no small feat.

To meet the various needs of our families, we provided child care so that a lack thereof would not be a barrier to attendance. We also always offered a full, warm dinner catered by a number of local restaurants, from a treasured soul food business down the street to a Spanish Caribbean restaurant owned by the family of one of our students, to ensure that the food we served reflected the diversity of our families and caregivers.

Taking a cue from circle practice's setting of guidelines and values, we always started our Community Conversations events by reviewing our norms: stay engaged, speak your truth, experience discomfort, and expect and accept non-closure. These norms, adapted from Glenn Singleton's *Courageous Conversations About Race* (2014), served as a reminder that difficult conversations can be uncomfortable, but that we can lean into rather than shy away from that discomfort. We articulated to our families that a handful of conversations each year was not going to solve, say, systemic racism, but what was important was being in community with each other, learning with and from one another, and giving each other permission to be our authentic selves. This was a powerful step toward repairing relationships, healing, and bringing our community together. We can say with confidence that universally designed cultures of restorative practices are effective mechanisms to both promote and facilitate healing because they were key to the healing of our own extraordinary school community.

44

Not Just One More Thing to Do

As educators, we are constantly being pulled in so many—*too many*—different directions. Competing responsibilities are often pitted against limited resources and time, and while we're busy juggling lesson plans, standardized assessments, and meeting after meeting, just to name a few, the students themselves can sometimes get lost in the mix. The frameworks of both UDL and restorative practices remind us that the work is and should always be student-centered. Utilizing these frameworks in concert shouldn't be viewed as adding one more item to an already full teaching to-do list, but as an approach that will actually result in more efficient and effective teaching and learning, genuine relationship-building, and authentic meaning-making for all.

As we conclude this exploration of UDL and restorative practices, the clear truth is that empowering and celebrating student voices can reshape education. We started with the understanding that education isn't just giving knowledge but an interactive exchange woven by mentorship, curiosity, and empathy. This exchange, often limited by traditional teaching, finds freedom in restorative practices. Student voices, often pushed to the sidelines, have a powerful impact. They spread thoughts and dreams, touching all corners of education. But these voices have been muted, suppressing innovation and insight. Through restorative practices, we've found a way to let these voices thrive. By encouraging dialogue and connection, we've seen a transformation in individuals and communities.

To all educators, we encourage you to continue this transformation. Let student voices be at the center of education. Let classrooms be places of collaboration and growth. By embracing restorative practices and prioritizing student voices, we can reshape schools and society. These conversations extend beyond classrooms, guiding us toward understanding and compassion and ultimately toward healing our broken school cultures and systems. Restorative practices remind us that there is no healing without a relationship, and UDL teaches us that there is no learning without a relationship.

45

Pause and Reflect On Part F

SUMMARY

In this chapter, we explored the principles of UDL—engagement, representation, and action and expression—alongside the restorative practices framework and saw their potential to create student-centered, equitable, and meaningful learning experiences. How might the merging of these frameworks empower educators to create more student-centered and equitable learning environments? Consider the concept of learner variability and its implications for embracing diverse strengths and weaknesses. How can educators strike a balance between standardized expectations and flexible support to foster genuine expertise among all students?

Finally, let's zoom out and contemplate the broader context. The intersection of UDL and restorative practices holds the potential to break down systemic barriers to education. Examine the decision-making processes in your educational setting. Whose voices are included, and whose perspectives might be inadvertently marginalized? How can we ensure that underrepresented voices—students, families, teachers—have an equal platform to contribute meaningfully to educational dialogue?

REFLECTION QUESTIONS

1. Delve into your teaching practices and ask yourself: How can I activate my students' intrinsic motivation through engagement strategies that resonate with their interests and needs?

2. Consider the role of student voice and agency in building a supportive and respectful classroom community. How can you integrate restorative circles and conferencing techniques to enhance engagement and deepen connections among students? Reflect on the impact of these practices on your students' emotional well-being and their readiness to learn.

3. How might you adapt your instructional materials and approaches to cater to student variability, ensuring that every student can access and comprehend the content?

4. How can you harness the combined power of UDL and restorative practices to cultivate a vibrant, student-centered, and equitable learning environment that empowers every learner to thrive?

A

The UDL Guidelines 3.0

The Universal Design for Learning Guidelines

The goal of UDL is **learner agency** that is purposeful & reflective, resourceful & authentic, strategic & action-oriented.

Design Multiple Means of Engagement

Design Options for Welcoming Interests & Identities
- Optimize choice and autonomy
- Optimize relevance, value, and authenticity
- Nurture joy and play
- Address biases, threats, and distractions

Design Options for Sustaining Effort & Persistence
- Clarify the meaning and purpose of goals
- Optimize challenge and support
- Foster collaboration, interdependence, and collective learning
- Foster belonging and community
- Offer action-oriented feedback

Design Options for Emotional Capacity
- Recognize expectations, beliefs, and motivations
- Develop awareness of self and others
- Promote individual and collective reflection
- Cultivate empathy and restorative practices

Design Multiple Means of Representation

Design Options for Perception
- Support opportunities to customize the display of information
- Support multiple ways to perceive information
- Represent a diversity of perspectives and identities in authentic ways

Design Options for Language & Symbols
- Clarify vocabulary, symbols, and language structures
- Support decoding of text, mathematical notation, and symbols
- Cultivate understanding and respect across languages and dialects
- Address biases in the use of language and symbols
- Illustrate through multiple media

Design Options for Building Knowledge
- Connect prior knowledge to new learning
- Highlight and explore patterns, critical features, big ideas, and relationships
- Cultivate multiple ways of knowing and making meaning
- Maximize transfer and generalization

Design Multiple Means of Action & Expression

Design Options for Interaction
- Vary and honor the methods for response, navigation, and movement
- Optimize access to assistive and accessible technologies and tools

Design Options for Expression & Communication
- Use multiple media for communication
- Use multiple tools for construction, composition, and creativity
- Build fluencies with graduated support for practice and performance
- Address biases related to modes of expression and communication

Design Options for Strategy Development
- Set meaningful goals
- Plan and anticipate challenges
- Organize information and resources
- Enhance capacity for monitoring progress
- Challenge exclusionary practices

Access | Support | Executive Function

ACKNOWLEDGMENTS

To Katie Novak, thank you for believing in me and having my back. To David Gordon and the team at CAST, thank you for making this book possible. To Pamela Chu-Sheriff, thank you for all that you've taught me throughout the years, for being such a great friend, colleague, co-leader, and now co-author. I wouldn't be where I am today had it not been for you. To Edgar Vasquez, the camaraderie we established back in 2003 has taken us a long way, and this is just the beginning of many more great things for us hood kids—let's show the world what we can accomplish when we believe in ourselves, our communities, the work, and each other.

—*Mirko*

Mirko, our journey together in the world of education is over a decade in the making, and thanks to this book, it looks like we're going to be stuck with each other for a little while longer! Through it all, I couldn't imagine a better thought partner, and I am so grateful for the unwavering support and vision you've gifted to me over the years. Thank you for everything, bro. Edgar, thank you for meeting me in that coffee shop all those years ago to talk all things RP. You set the stage for bringing this work to our school and for my own walk as a practitioner. Katie, you are a true testament to what a strong woman and a strong mama can do, which is anything! Thank you for leading the way and for all of the opportunities and encouragement you've provided for me. Lastly, thank you to everyone on the CAST team for lifting up this most important work.

—*Pam*

Mirko, one of VERY few individuals I consider an actual brother, it has been a journey! Over the course of a 20-year friendship, we have laughed, cried, and supported each other, and we continue to do so. I am looking forward to the next 20+ years to come. Pam, I was honored and humbled to have been able to work with you and alongside you with RP work. You have owned it and are living RP. Katie, the day I met you, you filled the space with your energy, charisma, and personality. You are such an honest and genuine person. I am honored to be allowed to be part of this project and such important work.

—Edgar

LAND ACKNOWLEDGMENT

Lastly, the field of restorative practices owes a huge debt to its original practitioners: various Indigenous peoples from around the world who have been engaged in this work since time immemorial. Restorative practices teach us that we must first name the harm that has been done before we can begin the work of repairing that harm. As a result, although we are coming to you in print, as Boston residents, we would be remiss if we did not also take time to acknowledge the land that we reside on. A land acknowledgment is a statement that recognizes Indigenous communities as the original inhabitants of the lands upon which an institution was built and currently occupies and operates in or where an event is being held. It is a way of respecting Indigenous people's long history in and their lasting connections to their traditional homelands.

We live on land that is the territory of the Massachusett, Pawtucket, Wampanoag, and Nipmuc peoples, who are the original stewards of this land. For over 400 years, their people, sovereignty, territory, and resources have been repeatedly violated and exploited. The innumerable acts of violence committed upon native peoples are evident not only in their murder, enslavement, and internment but also in the minimizing or complete erasure of native history, culture, and voices that still occurs to this day.

As people of color, we stand in solidarity and as allies in the struggle with our Indigenous brothers and sisters. However, as occupiers of this land, we must all recognize that this acknowledgment is just the first—not the final—step in the move toward healing and justice. As the authors of this text, we have been entrusted with a platform and a wide audience, and it is our duty to model both acknowledgment of harm and also taking action toward justice. As restorative practice practitioners, we want to reiterate that recognizing harm is just the starting point in moving the needle toward justice. Besides recognition and reflection, we encourage education and action by exploring some of the following resources or donating to these causes:

Learn more:

- Eastern Woodlands Rematriation, a collective of Indigenous womxn: https://rematriate.org
- Mashpee Wampanoag: https://mashpeewampanoagtribe-nsn.gov/culture
- Massachusett Tribe: http://massachusetttribe.org
- Massachusetts Center for Native American Awareness (MCNAA): https://www.mcnaa.org
- Massachusetts Commission on Indian Affairs: https://www.mass.gov/info-details/indian-affairs
- No Loose Braids, a Nipmuc-led organization: https://www.noloosebraids.com
- Wampanoag Tribe of Gay Head (Aquinnah): https://wampanoagtribe-nsn.gov/wampanoag-history

Donate:

- Eastern Woodlands Rematriation: https://whyhunger.org/ewrematriation
- Mashpee Wampanoag Tribe: https://mashpeewampanoagtribe-nsn.gov/donations
- Massachusetts Center for Native American Awareness (MCNAA): https://www.mcnaa.org/donate
- National Indigenous Women's Resource Center: https://www.niwrc.org/donate
- No Loose Braids Equinox Campaign: https://www.noloosebraids.com

REFERENCES

American Psychological Association Zero Tolerance Task Force. (2008). *Are zero tolerance policies effective in the schools? An evidentiary review and recommendations.* https://www.apa.org/pubs/info/reports/zero-tolerance.pdf

Anderson, M. (2016). *Learning to choose, choosing to learn: The key to student motivation and achievement.* ASCD.

Armour, M. (2012). Restorative justice: Some facts and history. *Tikkun, 27*(1), 25–65. https://doi.org/10.1215/08879982-2012-1012

Austin, R. D., & Williams, R. A. (2009). *Navajo courts and Navajo common law: A tradition of tribal self-governance.* University Of Minnesota Press.

Blake, C. (2015). *Teaching social justice in theory and practice.* https://education.cu-portland.edu/blog/classroom-resources/teaching-social-justice

Blood, P., & Thorsborne, M. (2005, March 3–5). *The challenge of culture change: Embedding restorative practice in schools* [Paper presentation]. Sixth International Conference on Conferencing, Circles and other Restorative Practices: Building a Global Alliance for Restorative Practices and Family Empowerment, Sydney, Australia.

Bloom, S. L. (2013). *Creating sanctuary: Toward the evolution of sane societies* (2nd ed.). Routledge.

Boyes-Watson, C., & Pranis, K. (2015). *Circle forward: building a restorative school community.* Living Justice Press.

Brasof, M., & Levitan, J. (2022). *Student voice research: Theory, methods, and innovations from the field.* Teachers College Press.

CASEL. (2024a). *Restorative practices and SEL alignment.* https://schoolguide.casel.org/uploads/sites/2/2020/12/2024.03_Aligning-SEL-and-RP-1.pdf

CASEL. (2024b). *SEL 3 signature practices playbook.* https://signaturepractices.casel.org

CASEL. (2024c). *What is the CASEL framework?* https://casel.org/fundamentals-of-sel/what-is-the-casel-framework

CAST. (2018). Universal Design for Learning Guidelines Version 2.2. http://udlguidelines.cast.org/more/downloads/

CAST. (2024). Universal Design for Learning Guidelines, Version 3.0. Author. http://udlguidelines.cast.org

Chardin, M., & Novak, K. (2020). *Equity by design: Delivering on the power and promise of UDL*. Corwin.

Cohen, G. L., & Steele, C. M. (2002). A barrier of mistrust. *Improving Academic Achievement*, 303–327. https://doi.org/10.1016/b978-012064455-1/50018-x

de Bono, E. (1985). *Six thinking hats*. Penguin Life.

Eccles, M. P., & Mittman, B. S. (2006). Welcome to implementation science. *Implementation Science*, *1*(1). https://doi.org/10.1186/1748-5908-1-1

Emdin, C. (2016). *For white folks who teach in the hood . . . and the rest of y'all too: Reality pedagogy and urban education*. Beacon Press.

Freire, P. (2000). *Pedagogy of the oppressed*. The Continuum International Publishing Group Inc.

Fullan, M. (2007). *The new meaning of educational change*. Teachers College Press.

Gabagambi, J. (2020, September). *A comparative analysis of restorative justice practices in Africa*. Hauser Global Law School Program. https://www.nyulawglobal.org/globalex/Restorative_Justice_Africa1.html

Ganz, M. (2009). *What is public narrative: Self, us & now (Public narrative worksheet)*. https://dash.harvard.edu/handle/1/30760283

Ganz, M. (2011, February 3). *Telling your public story: Self, us, now*. Issuu. https://issuu.com/wholecommunities/docs/public-story-worksheet07ganz/1

Gonzalez, J. (2017, October 3). *Meet the Single Point Rubric*. Cult of Pedagogy. https://www.cultofpedagogy.com/single-point-rubric

Gruenert, S., & Whitaker, T. (2017). *School culture recharged: Strategies to energize your staff and culture*. ASCD.

Hammond, Z. (2015). *Culturally responsive teaching and the brain: Promoting authentic engagement and rigor among culturally and linguistically diverse students*. Corwin.

Heifitz, R. A., & Linsky, M. (2002). *Leadership on the line: Staying alive through the dangers of leading*. Harvard Business Review Press.

Hodas, G. R. (2006, February). *Responding to childhood trauma: The promise and practice of trauma informed care*. Pennsylvania Office of Mental Health and Substance Abuse Services. https://www.nasmhpd.org/sites/default/files/2022-08/Responding%2520to%2520Childhood%2520Trauma%2520-%2520Hodas.pdf

Joe, C. M., Vaandering, D., Ricciardelli, R., Giwa, S., & Moore, S. (2022, July 10). *Two-eared listening is essential for understanding restorative justice in

Canada. The Conversation. https://theconversation.com/two-eared-listening-is-essential-for-understanding-restorative-justice-in-canada-185466#:~:text=Indigenous%20communities%20around%20the%20world

Kahne, J., Bowyer, B., Marshall, J., & Hodgin, E. (2022). Is responsiveness to student voice related to academic outcomes? Strengthening the rationale for student voice in school reform. *American Journal of Education*. https://doi.org/10.1086/719121

Kohl, H. (1994). *I won't learn from you: And other thoughts on creative maladjustment*. The New Press.

Marsh, V. (2017, June). *Restorative practice: History, successes, challenges & recommendations*. Center for Urban Education Success. https://www.rochester.edu/warner/cues/wp-content/uploads/2020/12/Restorative-Practices-Brief-1_marsh_final.pdf

Mehl-Madrona, L., & Mainguy B. (2014). Introducing healing circles and talking circles into primary care. *The Permanente Journal, 18*(2), 4–9. https://doi.org/10.7812/TPP/13-104

Meyer, J. F. (1998). History repeats itself: Restorative justice in Native American communities. *Journal of Contemporary Criminal Justice, 14*(1), 42–57.

Morrison, B. (2005, March 3–5). *Building safe and healthy school communities: Restorative justice and responsive regulation* [Paper presentation]. Sixth International Conference on Conferencing, Circles and other Restorative Practices: Building a Global Alliance for Restorative Practices and Family Empowerment, Sydney, Australia.

Museum of New Zealand. (n.d.). *Tokotoko tāniko (tāniko staff)*. https://collections.tepapa.govt.nz/object/1913914

National Implementation Research Network. (2020). *Implementation stages planning tool*. https://implementation.fpg.unc.edu/wp-content/uploads/Implementation-Stages-Planning-Tool.v8-NIRN-only-Fillable.pdf

Novak, K., & Couros, G. (2022). *UDL now!: A teacher's guide to applying universal design for learning*. Good Books.

Pranis, K. (2005). *The little book of circle processes: A new/old approach to peacemaking*. CAST Professional Publishing.

Pratt, J. (1996). Colonization, power and silence: A history of indigenous justice in New Zealand society. In B. Galaway & J. Hudson (Eds.), *Restorative justice: International perspectives* (pp. 137–155). Criminal Justice Press.

Schlechty, P. (2011). *Engaging students: The next level of working on the work*. Jossey-Bass.

Schwager, A., & Meyer, C. (2007, February). *Understanding customer experience*. Harvard Business Review. https://hbr.org/2007/02/understanding-customer-experience

Senge, P. M. (1990). *The fifth discipline: The art & practice of the learning organization*. Doubleday.

Shafer, L. (2018, July 23). *What makes a good school culture?* Harvard Graduate School of Education. https://www.gse.harvard.edu/ideas/usable-knowledge/18/07/what-makes-good-school-culture

Singleton, G. (2014). *Courageous conversations about race: A field guide for achieving equity in schools*. Corwin.

State Implementation and Scaling-up of Evidence-based Practices (SISEP). (2012). Implementation stages. https://sisep.fpg.unc.edu/

Stevenson, J. (1999). The circle of healing. *Native Social Work Journal, 2*(1), 8–21.

Tatum, B. (1997). *Why are all the black kids sitting together in the cafeteria? And other conversations about race*. Basic Books.

Tavares Avant, J. (2018, September 13). *Talking stick and feather: Indigenous tools hold sacred power of free speech*. ICT. https://ictnews.org/archive/talking-stick-and-feather-indigenous-tools-hold-sacred-power-of-free-speech

U.S. Department of Education Office for Civil Rights. (2014, March). *Civil rights data collection data snapshot: School discipline*. https://ocrdata.ed.gov/assets/downloads/CRDC-School-Discipline-Snapshot.pdf

Valandra, E. C. (Ed.). (2020). *Colorizing restorative justice: Voicing our realities*. Living Justice Press.

Visible Learning. (2018, March). *Collective teacher efficacy (CTE) according to John Hattie*. https://visible-learning.org/2018/03/collective-teacher-efficacy-hattie/

Wachtel, T. (2016, November). *Defining restorative*. International Institute for Restorative Practices. https://www.iirp.edu/images/pdf/Defining-Restorative_Nov-2016.pdf

Wachtel, T., & McCold, P. (2004, August 5). *Building a global alliance for restorative practices and family empowerment, Part 2*. The IIRP's Fifth International Conference on Conferencing, Circles and other Restorative Practices. Vancouver, Canada. https://www.iirp.edu/news/from-restorative-justice-to-restorative-practices-expanding-the-paradigm

White, S. (2012). *Time to think: Using restorative questions*. International Institute for Restorative Practices Graduate School. https://www.iirp.edu/news/time-to-think-using-restorative-questions

Windmuller-Luna, K. (2015). *Linguist staff: Ceremonial stool, chain, and swords motif (Ōkyeame poma)*. The Metropolitan Museum of Art. https://www.metmuseum.org/art/collection/search/315887

Yazzie, R., & Zion, J. W. (1996). Navajo restorative justice: The law of equality and justice. In B. Galaway & J. Hudson (Eds.), *Restorative justice: International perspectives* (pp. 157–173). Criminal Justice Press.

Zion, J. (1998). The dynamics of Navajo peacemaking. *Journal of Contemporary Criminal Justice, 14*(1), 58–74. https://doi.org/10.1177/1043986298014001005

INDEK

A
acceptance, 37
accountability, 66, 86
action and expression, 105, 205, 207–208, 227–228, 240
active listening
    in circle structure, 49, 141
    in Indigenous justice, 61
    life skill of, 28
    to personal narratives, 34
    and response to feedback, 86
    for talkative students, 103
    and talking pieces, 50–51
adaptive challenges, 161–162, 163
addition, 115
Adkins-Sharif, Jamel, EdD, JD, 163, 165
adults
    bias understood by, 177
    favoritism by, 187
    openness to feedback, 52
    and social discipline window, 59–60
advice from peers, 43
advisors/advisees, 187
advisory program, 33, 150, 153, 155
affective questions/statements, 47, 48
affirmations, 167
African traditions
    justice systems in, 63, 64
    personal narrative in, 127, 129
    rites of passage in, 73
    Ubuntu, 134, 166–167
agency, student
    authentic learning via, 4
    engagement and, 220
    equity via, 19
    exercise of, 117
    intentional practices for, 19
    and life skills, 204

    and previous trauma, 27
    proactive structures for, 13, 52
    restoring, 45, 144
    and social discipline window, 60
    success via, 24
    systems to ensure, 9
    in UDL tenets, 1
Akan people, 64
Algebra Project, 117
alienation, 149
American Bar Association, 70
American Journal of Education, 97
American Psychological Association, 70
amygdala, 22, 103
amygdala hijack, 142–145
ancestors, honoring, 73
apologies, 43–44, 90
assessment tools
    for action and expression, 207–208
    Beyond Access framework, 23
    self-assessment, 220
attendance rates, 13–14
attention, sustained, 207
authentic engagement, 206
authentic relevance, 22, 23, 112, 206–207, 221
awakening, in S.O.D.A strategy, 148

B
balance, as core school value, 8, 216, 217
barriers to learning, 143, 202, 204–205, 228–229
behavior/action
    normalizing racist, 65
    in school culture, 16
    and Story of Self, 150
    tangible evidence of, 16–17, 94

behaviors, unwanted
  circle practices for, 42–44, 166
  decreases in, 155
  disciplinary responses to, 17, 68
  Māori understanding of, 61
  restorative practices for, 88, 189, 195
  rites of passage program and, 73
  root causes of, 29, 61, 62
  and social discipline window, 60
  trauma lens on, 167, 179
belief systems, 4, 16
belonging
  case study of, 79–84
  in circle structure, 49
  equity via, 19
  learning via, 219
  in school culture, 17, 142
  UDL and RP for, 223
  voice and, 46
Beyond Access framework, 22, 23
bias
  addressed via UDL and RP, 222
  adult understanding of, 177
  implicit, 15
  systemic, 228–229
  unconscious, 65–66
  See also inequality; racism
Black men's circles, 133–134
Black Panthers, 172, 173
Black students, 67–69, 132, 178
Black women's circles, 134
blame, 51
blind spots, understanding, 23
body language, 140
boredom, 90–91
Boston Arts Academy, 31, 99, 100, 185, 186
Boston Public Schools (BPS), 3
boundaries, 59–60
brain function
  and the amygdala, 22, 103, 143
  in community, 199
  engagement and, 219–220
  safety and learning, 153, 219
  S.O.D.A. strategy for, 147–148
bravery, 22, 154
Burton, LeVar, 4
business world, 85

C
career pathways, 132, 203
caregivers
  and community feedback, 34
  diversity among, 231–232
  and social discipline window, 59–60
  structures for voice of, 232
CASEL (Collaborative for Academic, Social, and Emotional Learning), 124–125, 137–138, 157
  See also SEL (Social-Emotional Learning)
Center for Leadership and Educational Equity, 216
Center for Restorative Justice, 33
challenges
  normalizing, 24
  restorative practices to serve, 131
  in rolling out RJ, 175–176
  in Stories of Self, 55, 128, 150
  student voice on, 97
  technical and adaptive, 161–162
  UDL and RP for, 227
change
  of action from RP pilot, 190
  adaptive, 162, 171
  personal, 128
  in Stories of Self, 129, 150
  structural transformations, 235–236
  time required for, 161–162, 167, 171
check-in questions, 50, 211
check-out time, 50
choice
  in action and expression, 207–208
  choice boards, 207–208
  optimizing student, 209
  restorative practices and, 212
  in Stories of Self, 55, 128, 150
  in trauma-informed education, 18
  via UDL and RP, 221
  UDL and student, 212
circle practices
  belonging in, 28
  for Black men, 133–134
  and CASEL, 140, 141
  circle as symbol, 63

252   Index

community morning circles, 167–168
conflict resolution via, 174
content circles, 104, 105
derailment of, 175
effort/work to organize, 53
follow-up circles, 53–54
format and purpose of, 45
Indigenous systems of, 63
input on guidelines for, 51
norms for, 141
as ongoing, 101
openers, 43, 50, 105
peacemaking circles, 166–167
planning for, 42–43, 50, 51, 53
restorative justice and, 133–134
staff training in, 32
and Stories of Self, 154
student input on, 98, 99–100, 103
student-requested, 33
tiers of, 48
tips for running, 52–54
and valuing of diversity, 141
classrooms
changing dynamics in, 95
circles preceding time in, 101
cogens to improve, 94
piloting restorative practices in, 33
as safe space, 103
school culture in, 15–16
segregation in, 132
student feedback on, 88
student voice in, 188
walk-throughs of, 205
Clinton, President Bill, 67
Clock Partners, 145
closings, intentional, 50, 145–146
cogenerative dialogues
cultivating belonging via, 28
example of, 88–91
as formal RP structure, 47
goal of, 55, 87
opting out of, 93
steps to implementing, 93–95
student agency via, 87–88, 119
collaboration, 142–143
collective teacher efficacy, 34
collectivism
in circle structure, 49

collective memory carriers, 127
in Indigenous justice, 61–64
restorative practice framework
of, 46
via UDL and RP, 222
colonialism, 61, 62, 64–65
Colorizing Restorative Justice: Voicing Our Realities (Valandra), 46
communication, 140
community
circles to build, 49, 101, 134, 167–168
collaborative, 18
of families/caregivers, 232–233
griot tradition in, 128
healing in, 44
Indigenous wisdom on, 61–64, 168–169
members of school community, 34
practices to develop, 1, 45, 140, 219
and restorative justice, 133, 177
restorative practices called in by, 173
and school culture, 15
sense of belonging in, 46
and Ubuntu, 134
UDL and RP for, 223
vision, values, and voice input, 215–218
community-building circles
power of, 173–174
vs. repair circles, 49
in RP tier structure, 56, 57
work required for, 53
Community Conversations, 34, 232–233
confidentiality, 51
conflict resolution
addressing root causes in, 61, 62
after community-building, 134–135
circle practices for, 166, 174
in community, 44
de-escalation skills for, 190
Indigenous systems of, 61–64
and individual self-esteem, 74
mechanisms in place for, 24–25, 31
and open conversation, 28
and relationship skills, 139
restorative practices for, 1, 45
student voice in, 13, 27
trauma and, 73

Index   253

content circles, 104, 105
continuous learning
    for authentic RP work, 65–66
    fostering a culture of, 22
    on trauma, 19
control, in social discipline window, 59–60
conversation, open
    belonging via, 28
    cogens as, 87, 95
    impromptu, 47, 48
    for parents/caregivers, 194, 232–233
    restorative practice of, 37, 173
    schoolwide, 194
Courageous Conversations About Race (Singleton), 233
COVID-19 pandemic, 37, 38
creativity, 105, 202
criminal justice system
    restorative justice in, 2, 46, 70
    school-to-prison pipeline, 67, 68
cultural considerations
    in cogens, 87, 93
    and cross-cultural competence, 65–66
    and school diversity, 18
    and social awareness, 141
Culturally Responsive Teaching and the Brain, 147
cultural self-esteem, 73
culture, school
    blind spots in, 23
    of continuous improvement, 22
    defined, 13, 15
    five elements of, 16
    inclusive/safe, 13
    intentionality in, 17
    restorative practices in, 14, 34, 48
    as school-specific, 162
    stories of self in, 152
    strengthening, 141
    time required to change, 161–162, 171, 178, 180
    transforming unhealthy, 11, 37
    trauma-informed, 19
    vision, values, and voice in, 215–218
curriculum
    circles as part of, 104
    hidden curriculum, 15
    restorative practices in, 192–193
customer service, 81, 85, 88, 91
Cutler, Kareem, 105, 109

D

Davis, Fania, 131, 172
decision-making
    in CASEL framework, 125, 127, 138, 139, 157
    circle practices for, 50
    and individual counsel, 168
    schoolwide, 229
    student voice in, 27, 98
decolonization, 169
de-escalation skills, 190
DESE (Massachusetts Department of Elementary and Secondary Education), 3, 34, 154, 168
detachment, 147–148
dialogue
    cogenerative, 55, 87–95
    math, 109–113
    in productive circles, 52
    RJ as a method for, 179
    student voice in, 98
disability status, 68
disciplinary actions. *See* punitive actions
disciplinary hearings, 187, 188, 189, 190, 195
discipline, in social discipline window, 59–60
discussion rounds, 43, 50, 53
distrust, trauma and, 28, 73
diversity
    circles and valuing of, 141
    in cogen group, 93
    of families/caregivers, 231–232
    sensitivity to cultural, 18
    UDL and RP for, 226
Do Now/Activators, 43, 105, 106, 145

E

education
    antiracist, 177
    as art, not science, 162
    authentic relevance in, 22

    circle use in, 103–106
    in core skills, 203–204
    decolonizing, 169
    intention vs. impact of, 9
    and narrative, 129
    shifting methods of, 4
    student-centric, 1–2, 9, 235–236
    and student interest, 2
educators
    buy-in for RP programs, 190–192
    cogens with students, 87
    collective teacher efficacy, 34
    diversity among, 8
    favoritism by, 187
    inspiration to become, 107, 123–124
    responsibilities of, 15, 27
    RP as improving, 110
    RP education for, 32, 57, 192–194
    in schoolwide decisions, 229
    as serving students, 1–2, 81, 85–86
    staffing shortages, 14
elementary settings, 166
Emdin, Dr. Christopher, 55, 87, 149
Emerging Leaders, 100
emotions
    and the amygdala hijack, 143
    emotional intelligence, 128
    and engagement, 220
    and isolation, 132
    and learning, 103
    post-trauma, 28
    regulation of, 28, 29
    and safe learning conditions, 143–144
    S.O.D.A. strategy for, 147
    statements/questions about, 47, 48
empathy, 28, 66, 128, 189, 220, 225
empowerment
    in circle structure, 52
    and honoring student voice, 98
    via math dialogue, 112–113
    via restorative practices, 27, 29, 37, 140
    via storytelling, 128
    in trauma-informed education, 18, 19
engagement
    learning activated by, 219–220
    levels of student, 93, 205–207
    and perseverance, 20
    in processing answers, 109, 111
    and respect for identity, 149
    restorative practices and, 33–34, 220–225
    and RP rollout, 193
    in SEL 3, 145
    and student voice, 97, 105
    in UDL framework, 105, 205, 220, 240
    and valuing student feedback, 90–91
    walk-throughs for, 206–207
    as the "why," 205
equality
    and authentic RP work, 177–178
    via belonging/agency, 19
    in circles, 50
    in education/career options, 132–133
    healing via, 14, 37
    proactive frameworks for, 13
    racial, 135–136
    and removing barriers, 228–229
    student outcomes as test of, 24
    via UDL and RP, 228
exclusion, 79–84, 190, 228
executive function, 152, 153, 207, 227
expectations, goals and, 203, 223, 237
exploration stage for RP, 181–183, 187–189
expulsion, 67–69, 124

F

facilitators
    for circle practice, 50, 53
    of cogens, 93–95
    in Indigenous justice systems, 64
    of peacemaking circles, 166
    students as RP, 193–194
    student-selection by, 111
    for tier 2/3 approaches, 57
families/parents
    and community feedback, 34
    customer service for, 85–86
    diversity among, 231–232
    RP and conversations with, 194
    RP feedback from, 195
    and social discipline window, 59–60

families/parents (*continued*)
    structures for voice of, 232
Farese, Dr. Christina, 147, 149
feedback
    about racial/cultural issues, 66
    adult openness to, 52
    via cogens, 87
    from entire school community, 34
    equity audits, 19
    and individual self-esteem, 74
    mechanisms for, 14
    protocols for discussing, 216
    responding to student, 85–86, 97–98
    on RP rollout, 195
    on Stories of Self, 151–152
    via UDL and RP, 223
    valuing student, 88, 90–91
The Fifth Discipline: The Art & Practice of the Learning Organization (Senge), 24
fight, flight, or freeze response, 80–81, 143
Fiji, 71–72
First Harm, 65
First Nations people, 63
fishbowls, 32
food, access to, 136
formal restorative practices
    cogenerative dialogues, 87–91
    overview of, 55–58
    in RP tier structure, 47
Freire, Paolo, 2

G

Ganz, Marshall, 55, 127, 128–129, 150
gender, punitive action and, 68
goals
    of circle practices, 50
    for school culture, 215
    UDL and firm, 202, 203
    via UDL and RP, 223, 227
Godfrey, Chris, 105–107, 115, 119
Goens-Bradley, Sharon, 65
griot (storyteller), 127
group discussions, 28
guidelines, circle, 50
Gun-Free Schools Act, 67
Guthrie, Sean, 71

H

Hammond, Zaretta, 147, 149, 199
happiness, 60, 221
harm, repairing
    in community, 44
    via consequences, 44
    derailment of, 176–177
    Indigenous systems of, 61–64
    mechanisms in place for, 24–25
    piloting RP in, 189–190
    repair circles, 49
    via restorative justice, 2, 61–64, 70
    restorative practices for, 1, 27–29, 45
    student options for, 195
    time required for, 53–54
Harvard University, 55
Hattie, John, 34
healing
    case study of need for, 11–13
    in a circle, 63
    in community, 44
    dialogue as empowering, 112–113
    of First Harm, 65
    Indigenous communal, 61–64
    and individual self-esteem, 74
    in juvenile justice system, 31
    recognizing need for, 13, 14
    restorative practices for, 27–29, 34, 147
    via rites of passage, 73
    of school culture, 18–19, 24–25, 37
    and school uniqueness, 162
    and shifting mindsets, 165–166
    time required for, 13, 53–54, 161–162, 171, 178, 180
Henderson, James Sákéj Youngblood, 77
hidden curriculum, 15
Hooker, David Anderson, 178
hooks, bell, 1
human rights, 140
humility, 66

I

icebreaker activities, 53
identity development
    for authentic RP work, 65–66
    as a Black man, 133–134

CASEL framework for, 125, 140
and connecting with roots, 71
and engagement, 220
for families/caregivers, 232-233
and individual self-esteem, 73, 74
learning and mutual respect, 149
and mutual sharing, 117
stories of self, 55-56, 117, 153
ignored, being, 83
impact
    impact vs. intent, 9, 17, 22, 23, 89
    measuring school culture's, 19
    in restorative practices, 47
    of trauma, 21
implementation of RP
    case study of, 185-195
    stages of, 181-183
impromptu conversations, 47, 48
incarceration, 68, 131
inclusion, 142-143, 144-145, 228, 229
Indigenous traditions
    basic human rights in, 140
    circles in, 63
    and colonialism, 61, 62, 64
    on community, 168-169
    co-opting of, 178
    personal narrative in, 127
    of restorative justice, 61-63
    restorative practices in, 35, 46, 75, 140
    Talking Stick in, 64
individualized interventions, 55, 168, 179
inequality
    and food access, 136
    reinforcement of, 203
    systemic, 65-66, 228-229
initiative fatigue, 181
In Schools We Trust, 133
installation of RP, 181-183, 189-191
intensive mediation, 56
intent and impact, 9, 13, 89
intentionality
    as needed for healing, 14
    in restorative practice use, 34
    in school culture, 17
    in SEL 3, 145-146
    in social justice work, 177

International Institute for Restorative Practices (IIRP), 33, 138
interruption, 51, 100
invisibility
    racism and, 79-84
    student experience of, 90, 119
isolation, 28, 132

J

judgment, 13, 51, 168
justice, restorative. See restorative justice
justice systems
    Indigenous, 61-64
    juvenile, 31, 68, 172
    restorative justice in, 2
    and RJOY, 131
juvenile justice system, 31, 68, 172

K

Kahne, Dr. Joseph, 97
Kennedy School of Government, 55
Kinga people, 63
Kohl, Herbert, 149

L

Lang, Dr. Gaye, 65
language acquisition, 140
Lawrence-Lightfoot, Dr. Sara, 149
leadership
    initiatives for young people, 117
    and patience, 167
    responsibilities of school, 89
    shared, in circles, 50
    three requirements for, 168
learners (adult and children)
    agency for, 24
    sense of belonging for, 46
    vulnerability modeled by, 98
learning
    and the amygdala hijack, 143
    authentic, 2, 4
    circle use in, 103-104
    community for, 219
    goals, 202
    and lack of relationship, 149
    removing barriers to, 1, 143, 204-205
    safe space for, 103

Index   **257**

learning (continued)
　　via Stories of Self, 155
　　and student interest, 207, 219-220
lessons vs. mistakes, 43, 44
Lewis, Ayo, 131
libations, 63, 73
life skills
　　CASEL framework of, 125, 139-140, 157
　　communication as, 140
　　to deal with trauma, 18
　　making connections, 116
　　restorative practices for, 27, 29
　　via SEL, 128
　　top 10 for 2025, 203-204
limbic system, 22
Locust, Dr. Carol, 64
low-stakes prompts, 43

M

male students, rites of passage for, 73-74
Maori justice system, 61, 64
marginalized groups, 65, 68, 98, 163, 203, 221, 223, 237
Massachusetts Department of Secondary and Elementary Education, 5, 34, 154, 168
math education
　　circle use in, 105-106
　　comprehension/connections in, 116, 117
　　hating math, 115, 116
　　Math Talks, 109-113
　　teacher inspiration for, 107
Math Talks, 105, 109-113
Mbiti, J.S., 159
MCAS tests, 41
meaning making, 226
memory, 127, 143
mental health services, 167
microaggressions, 132
middle school, 149, 153
Mindful Minute Brain Break, 145
mindsets, shifting, 163, 168, 176
mistakes, lessons vs., 43, 44
morale, student, 17

Moses, Bob, 117
multiplication, 115

N

narrative sharing
　　and decision-making, 139
　　between educators, 123-125
　　healing communities via, 147
　　restorative practice of, 28, 34
　　school-wide, 124
　　and SEL, 119, 150
　　Story of Self model, 55, 128-129
National Implementation Research Network, 181
Native American justice systems, 62, 63
Native American students, 67-69
Navajo judicial system, 62
neglect, 59-60
New Hope Youth Coalition, 31
next-generation skills, 203-204
Nigerian justice systems, 63
norms
　　for circle practice, 141
　　for community conversations, 233
　　for Math talks, 110
　　modeling vulnerability as, 116
　　in school culture, 16
Novak, Katie, 201
nurture
　　of joy/play, 221
　　and social discipline window, 59-60
　　student support by staff, 187
　　three conditions of, 142-143

O

Oakland Unified School District (OUSD), 132, 171, 172, 181
observation, 147-148
openers, 43, 50, 105
opting out, 93
outcomes
　　in Stories of Self, 55, 150
　　values, practices, and, 24
ownership of personal action
　　as core school value, 8, 216, 217
　　healing/repair via, 27-29

P

paradigm shifts, 46, 74
parents. *See* families/parents
passion, as core school value, 7, 216–217
patience, 135, 141, 167, 175
pausing/stopping, emotions and, 147–148
peacemaking, 62, 135, 166–167
Pedagogy of the Oppressed (Freire), 2
peers
    advice from, 43
    harm repair amidst, 44
    restorative circles with, 42–43
    supportive, 18
    trust in, 52
people of color
    Black men's circles, 133
    and decolonizing education, 169
    in the education system, 2
    racism and invisibility, 79–84
    RJ and justice for, 177
permissiveness, 59–60
perseverance
    in circle practice, 175
    as core school value, 8, 216, 217
    and engagement, 220
    school culture of, 22
personal journeys
    in changing educational models, 4
    restorative practices to serve, 28, 135
    in stories of self, 128–129
perspective taking, 48
Platform for the New Economy and Society, 203
polls, student/faculty, 8–9
power, 66, 168
practices, values, outcomes, and, 24
pride, as core school value, 7, 216, 217
Private Think-Time, 145
privilege, 66, 94
progress, monitoring, 227
punitive actions
    and colonialism, 61, 62, 64
    vs. community healing, 44
    exclusion as, 190
    historic move away from, 70
    as operating basis, 17
    racial statistics on, 67–69
    restorative practices vs., 46, 174
    and retraumatization, 28
    and student voice, 186–187, 188
    suspension, 12
Putnam Avenue Upper School, 3, 7, 29, 55, 71, 105, 116, 123, 147, 150, 154, 185, 201, 212, 215, 230

Q

questions
    affective, 47, 48
    check-in, 50, 211
    check-out, 50
    scaffolding, 111–112
    tier 2/3 restorative, 57–58

R

racial justice
    and RJOY, 131
    RJ practices and, 177, 178
    RP work for, 65–66, 135–136, 171
    for students of color, 132
    and trauma-informed education, 179
racism
    as felt by students, 132
    institutionalized, 15, 65–66, 177
    investigating personal/implicit, 65–66
    and invisibility, 79–84
    punitive action statistics and, 67–69
    RJ and undoing structures of, 177
    stress of, 80–81
Reading Rainbow, 4
rebellion, 206
rebuilding relationships, 56
reconciliation, 63
reentry meetings, 56
reflection/reflective practices
    in circles, 104
    before cogens, 88
    fostering a climate for, 48
    learner agency and, 204
    Math Talks as, 109–110
    open conversation, 37
    and personal improvement plans, 106
    Think, Ink, Pair, Share, 145
    via UDL and RP, 224

relationships
    advisor/advisee, 187
    among diverse families, 232-233
    and check-in questions, 211
    cross-cultural, 65
    healing, 9-10
    learning in, 236
    rebuilding, 56, 57
    repairing, 56, 57
    restorative practices for, 27, 29, 45, 219
    skills, 50, 125, 127, 138, 139, 157
    and social discipline window, 59-60
    and stories of self, 152
    student/faculty, 8, 17
    and trust in circles, 52
relevance, authentic, 22, 23
repair circles
    vs. community-building circles, 49
    high-leverage students in, 52
    over time, 53-54
    as tier 2 practice, 56, 57
    willingness for, 52-53
representation
    of community voice, 218
    learner, 22, 23
    restorative practices and, 226
    in UDL framework, 105, 205, 207, 240
respect, mutual
    in Indigenous justice, 61
    learning and, 149
    trauma and lack of, 73
    and trauma-informed education, 27
    UDL and RP for, 226
Responding to Childhood Trauma (Hodas), 19
restorative circles. See circle practices
restorative conferences, 33, 42, 47, 56, 90
restorative justice
    and Black student advocacy, 132-134
    in the criminal justice system, 2
    financial considerations, 175-176
    goal of, 136
    grassroots nature of, 176
    Indigenous systems of, 61-64
    in juvenile justice system, 31
    in Oakland Unified School District, 171-172
    for/by peers, 174-175
    restorative practices and, 45, 132
    and RJOY, 131
    and SEL, 179
    and social equality, 135-136
    Western beginnings of, 70
restorative practices
    and CASEL, 137-138, 140, 142, 144, 157
    case study of implementing, 185-195
    circle practices, 49-54
    cogenerative dialogues as, 87-95
    colonizing, 64-65
    community call for, 173
    components of, 28
    continuum of, 47-48
    culturally authentic, 65-66
    defined, 1, 45, 75, 142
    engagement and, 220-225
    formal structures, 55-59
    healing via, 24-25, 27-29, 37
    implementation of, 181-183, 192, 197
    and individual self-esteem, 74
    level playing field for, 66
    Math Talks, 109-113
    as mindset/paradigm shift, 46, 163, 168, 176, 185
    philosophy of, 173
    piloting of, 33, 189
    preparations for, 176-177, 178
    and restorative justice, 45-46
    safe/inclusive culture via, 14
    and school uniqueness, 162
    staff training in, 32-33, 57, 192
    for student agency/voice, 19, 97-98, 119, 212
    tier format for, 56-57, 75
    time required for, 162, 165
    UDL lens for, 202, 211-213, 219-230, 237
    as voluntary, 179
    See also specific practice by name
retraumatization, 27, 28

retreatism, 206
rites of passage, 73-74
ritual compliance, 206
RJOY (Restorative Justice for Oakland Youth), 131, 172
Rosebud Sioux Reservation, 65
rules, emphasis on, 12

S

safe spaces
    circles as, 49
    classrooms as, 16, 103
    creating, 29
    vs. exclusion/invisibility, 79-84
    to express thought process, 109-111
    healing in, 166
    restorative practices for, 140
    in school culture, 19
    in trauma-informed education, 18-19, 21
safety
    addressed via UDL and RP, 222
    as condition of nurture, 142-143
    lack of, 8, 12, 13, 166
    learning via, 153, 219
    in restorative practices and SEL, 142
    in school culture, 13
    in sharing stories of self, 154
Sankofa Rites of Passage program, 73-74
scaffolding, 111-112, 203
schools
    core values for, 7-8
    inconsistency across, 187-188
    picture of unhealthy, 11-13
school shootings, 67
school-to-prison pipeline, 68, 177
security guards, 67, 135
segregation, 132
SEL (Social-Emotional Learning)
    CASEL 5, 125, 138-142, 157
    circle practices for, 50, 157
    defined, 137, 142
    individual challenges in, 55
    life skills via, 128
    mutual sharing in, 119
    RP and, 137-138, 142, 179, 193
    and safe classrooms, 103
    schoolwide, 142
    and Stories of Self, 127-129, 149-155
    three signature practices in, 144-145
self-awareness
    in CASEL framework, 50, 125, 138, 157
    and emotion, 144
    and hearing others, 141
    restorative justice and, 136
    restorative practices for, 227
    and SEL 3, 146
    success via, 144
    via UDL and RP, 224
self-esteem, 73, 74, 110
self-management, 50, 125, 127, 138, 157
self-regulation, 207
Senge, Peter, 24
setbacks to healing, 53-54
Shafer, Leah, 16
shame, 51
Sherrod, Barbara, 46
Singleton, Glenn, 233
Sista Cypher, 134
snacks, offering, 94
social awareness, 50, 125, 127, 128, 137, 138, 141, 144, 157, 224
social discipline window, 59-60
social justice
    and authentic RP work, 65-66, 177-178
    in criminal system, 2
    restorative practices and, 171, 178
    student voice on, 97
S.O.D.A. (Stop. Observe. Detach. Awaken.) strategy, 147-148
S-Q-F (Single Quiet File), 12
Story of Self activities
    decision-making and, 139
    for educators, 123-125
    empowerment via, 128
    for families/caregivers, 232
    feedback on, 151-152
    as formal RP structure, 47
    healing communities via, 147
    learning via, 155
    restorative justice and, 133-134

Story of Self activities (*continued*)
  school-wide, 34, 116, 124, 153–154, 155
  and SEL, 149–155
  strengths/weaknesses in, 117
Story of Self Day, 153–155
storytelling, 64, 127
strategic compliance, 206
strengths-based approach, 18
stress
  and the amygdala hijack, 22, 103, 143
  of racism, 80–81
  in trauma-informed education, 18
strictness, 59–60
student/educator relationship
  collaboration in, 119
  favoritism in, 187
  fostering healthy, 17
  sharing stories in, 116
  strengthening, 141
  student voice in, 186–188
  trust in, 52
students
  attendance by, 13–14
  centering of, 202, 235–236
  as co-creators, 2, 28, 95, 209, 235–236
  communication skills for, 140
  customer service for, 85–86
  dislike of school by, 9, 12
  feeling of belonging for, 17
  gaining trust of, 16
  math dialogue by, 109–113
  modern challenges for, 2
  piquing interest of, 105
  relationships with adults, 59–60
  representation for, 22, 23
  safe/welcoming spaces for, 81–82
  with social capital, 52
  students of color, 67–69, 132, 177–178
  trauma and dysregulated, 167
  treated as criminals, 67
  valuing of, 88
  variability among, 202–203
  voice of. See voice, student
success
  academic and social, 152–153, 155
  via centering voice, 34
  via learner agency, 24
  in RP implementation, 181–183
  and self-awareness, 144
  in Stories of Self, 150–152
Successful Practices Network (SPN), 8
Suffolk University, 33
support of students
  favoritism in, 187
  flexibility in, 203, 237
  and social discipline window, 59–60
  for students of color, 133
  for trauma, 18–19
suspension
  goal of reduced, 189, 191
  restorative practices vs., 46
  RP and decreased, 155, 178
  and sense of belonging, 17
  for students of color, 67
  in unhealthy environments, 12
sustained attention, 207

T

talking pieces, 43, 50, 141
Tanzania, 63
targeted practices, 56
Tatum, Dr. Beverly, 149
teaching. See education
technical challenges, 161
tension build-up, 100, 190
tests, 41, 106
Think, Ink, Pair, Share, 145
tier 1 approaches
  circles as, 32, 47
  as first, 134
  Math Talks in, 111
  proactive strengthening of, 58, 75
  in RP tier structure, 56–57
tier 2 approaches, 47, 56–57, 212
tier 3 approaches, 56, 57
toxic environments, 13, 52
transition activities, 98
trauma
  action and expression in, 207
  effects of collective, 21
  emotions following, 28
  of First Harm, 65
  global, 37

healing circles for, 63
retraumatization, 27, 28
and self-esteem, 73, 74
trauma-informed education, 18–19, 27–29, 176–177, 179
and unwanted behaviors, 167, 179
trust
    and awareness of impact, 17
    in circle practice, 52
    via community-building, 134–135
    lack of, 8
    in response to feedback, 86
    in RP rollout, 190, 191, 193
    in safe spaces, 16, 29
    in trauma-informed education, 18
    and voice, 46
truth, perspective as, 141

U

Ubuntu, 134, 166–167
UDL (Universal Design for Learning)
    action and expression in, 205
    and barriers to learning, 143
    basic framework of, 105
    engagement in, 205–207
    Guidelines 3.0, 220, 221–228, 240
    overview of, 1, 201–209, 237
    proactive DEI via, 13
    representation in, 205, 207
    and restorative practices, 211–213, 237
    RP implementation and, 185–186
    student choice/voice in, 212
UDL Now!: A Teacher's Guide to Applying Universal Design for Learning in Today's Classrooms (Novak), 201
United States, First Harm done by, 65
universal restorative practices, 56–57
unseen, being, 12–13, 17
U.S. Department of Education Office for Civil Rights, 68

V

Valandra, Dr. Edward C., 46, 65
values
    CASEL framework to develop, 125
    circles and shared, 50
    practices, and outcomes, 24
    and school culture, 7–8, 15, 16
    and Story of Self, 150, 153
    student portfolios on, 218
    vision, values, and voice, 215–218
variability
    action and expression and, 207–208
    designing for, 24
    in RP implementation, 186
    UDL and learner, 11, 202–203, 237
Vasquez, Edgar, 31, 32, 100
victim-offender mediation, 70
violence, 67, 73, 131, 176
vision, values, and voice, 215–218
voice, student
    agency and, 1
    authentic learning via, 4, 97, 119
    case studies lacking, 12
    centering, 34, 112
    in classrooms, 188
    via cogens, 87, 93–95
    in education research, 97–101
    empowering, 52
    engagement and, 220
    responding to, 86, 88, 97–98, 235–236
    restorative practices and, 212
    and staff favoritism, 187
    systems to ensure, 9, 13, 14, 91, 98
    UDL and centering of, 202, 209
voice(s)
    amplifying unheard, 37
    and collectivist paradigm, 46
    equity for family/caregiver, 232
    inclusion of all, 50–51, 228–229
    restoring agency and, 45
    supporting adult, 14
    in tier 2/3 approaches, 57
    vision, values, and voice, 215–218
volunteers, diverse, 93
vulnerability, modeling
    via cogens, 98
    and healing school culture, 165
    by leadership, 66, 86, 168
    normalizing, 197
    in safety, 154, 155
    in stories of self, 116, 128, 151

W

Walker, Alice, 39
welcome
    in circle structure, 49
    and connecting with roots, 71–72
    in customer service, 85–86
    and engagement, 220
    and exclusion, 79–84
    school culture of, 19, 21
    in SEL 3, 144–145
WE Learn/WE Teach, 8
Western society, 61, 62, 64–65, 70
White, Michael, 178
White people, 66, 132
White students, 68
white supremacy, 37, 65–66
willingness, in productive circles, 52–53

Y

Yazzie, Chief Justice Emeritus Robert, 62
Young People's Project, 117
Yusem, David, 171

Z

zero tolerance policies, 67, 68, 70
Zion, James, 62

ABOUT THE AUTHORS

Mirko Chardin is Novak Education's Chief Equity and Inclusion Officer. Before joining Novak, he was the Founding Head of School of the Putnam Avenue Upper School in Cambridge, MA. Mirko's work has involved all areas of school management and student support. His greatest experience and passion revolve around culturally connected teaching and learning, recruiting and retaining educators of color, restorative practice, and school culture. Mirko presents both locally and nationally on issues of cultural proficiency, equity, Universal Design for Learning, and the use of personal narratives. He is also the co-author, with Dr. Katie Novak, of the bestselling *Equity by Design: Delivering on the Power and Promise of UDL*. He is available to provide workshops, seminars, and training on implicit bias, microaggressions, UDL, restorative practice, identity, courageous conversations about race, and personal narratives.

Pamela Chu-Sheriff is currently a consultant with Novak Educational Consulting, where she provides keynotes, workshops, and coaching for school leaders and staff, both in and outside of the United States, on topics ranging from UDL and restorative practices to equity and school leadership. Prior to her time at Novak, Pam served as a teacher and leader in urban education for nearly 20 years. She was a founding administrator of a diverse public middle school in Cambridge, MA, and also served in the Boston Public Schools as a school leader and an English and Humanities teacher at both the middle and high school levels. The proud daughter of Taiwanese immigrants, she has provided antiracism workshops for nonprofit organizations and universities and was a board member of the Asian American Resource Workshop. Pam holds a BA from Tufts University and an MEd from the Harvard Graduate School of Education. Pam enjoys all things food-related as well as spending time with her husband and daughter.

Edgar Vasquez has over 20 years of experience as an exemplary educator in the Boston Public Schools (BPS). He has been a pioneer in the Circle Practice and Restorative Justice framework and implementation in BPS. He is continuously sharing his knowledge, wisdom, best practices, and expertise in dismantling the school-to-prison pipeline by holding workshops, training, and professional development for other educators in the New England area to develop restorative practices and equity for all students.

In his current role, he serves as a school administrator as the founding dean of students at the only public arts school in Boston, where he's become a stronger school leader and school administrator. He is passionate about working with adolescents who are often misheard, misinterpreted, and looked down upon. He helps to mold students and encourages them to make their points clearly and respectfully, regardless of any obstacles that may be present. His expertise comes in working with adolescents from all ages but more specifically with adolescents whom society deems as troubled teens. His career has been working with adolescent-age students in middle and high school.

www.ingramcontent.com/pod-product-compliance
Lightning Source LLC
Chambersburg PA
CBHW070051080526
44586CB00013B/1003